inspired
cable knits

inspired cable knits

20 Creative Designs for Making Sweaters and Accessories

FIONA ELLIS

POTTER
CRAFT

New York

Photography copyright © by Lindsey Maier, except images noted below.

The photographs identified on the following pages are copyright © 2005 by Jupiter Images and its Licensors. All rights reserved. p. 2 (tree at upper left, butterfly on lower right); p. 16 (leaves at upper right; butterfly on left of second row, upper right; caterpillar on third row, right; fall leaves on lower right; pupa on lower left); p. 48 (tree roots at upper right; tree bark in middle row, right; tree bark on right of middle row, left); p. 78 (coil on middle left; lightning bolt at top middle; sand ripples in lower middle); p. 93 (sand ripples on lower right); p. 108 (woman on rocks on lower left); back cover (leaves at upper left; sand ripples on lower left).

Published in the United States by Potter Craft,
an imprint of the Crown Publishing Group,
a division of Random House, Inc., New York.
www.crownpublishing.com
www.clarksonpotter.com

POTTER CRAFT and CLARKSON N. POTTER
are trademarks, and POTTER and colophon are
registered trademarks of Random House, Inc.

Every effort has been made to ensure that the instructions in this book are accurate and complete. We cannot be responsible for variance of individual knitters, human errors, or typographical mistakes.

Library of Congress Cataloging-in-Publication Data is available

ISBN 1-4000-8061-4

Printed in Singapore

Design by Caitlin Daniels Israel

10 9 8 7 6 5 4 3 2 1

First Edition

contents

introduction

It is a powerful and intense moment when an artist realizes that she can strike a chord with another individual through her chosen form of expression. During the conception of *Inspired Cable Knits,* I discovered that I had the power not only to strike a chord, but to make the whole band play. But this would be no unplugged set; I would be tapping into the power and wisdom of Mother Nature herself. The four concepts I explore in this book are:

inspired by change

THE ORGANIC EVOLUTION OF PATTERNS

inspired by nature

THE BEAUTY IN TREE BARK

inspired by energy

THE FORCES WITHIN OUR WORLD

inspired by time

THE VALUE OF SLOWING DOWN

As in a traditional knitting book, *Inspired Cable Knits* contains a collection of patterns. The projects themselves are contemporary cable knits, modern classics. I also wanted to throw light on the creative process, so I have included written and visual material that reflects my design philosophy. To address the contemplative nature of knitting, you will find mindfulness pointers included with each pattern. These are suggestions to focus on or to ponder during the knitting process.

I have been in love with cable knits for as long as I can remember. I love their crunchy, nubbly textures. Ever since I began designing sweaters professionally, I have been experimenting with new and different ways to use traditional patterns. I wanted to retain their appeal while pushing the boundaries of interest in knitting them. Not to make them more complicated or demanding to knit, just more engaging. Each twist is a building block that contributes to something much more beautiful than the sum of its parts.

I love to knit; that's a given. I also love going to author readings, gallery openings, and film festivals, obviously for the material shown, but mostly for the question-and-answer sessions that follow—for these often reveal the artist's initial spark of inspiration. I have also discovered that when I give presentations, the audience invariably becomes most animated when the questions move toward how I came up with an idea for a design. We relish the opportunity to identify with the unique insights offered by artists, not only for enjoyment, but also for the purpose of educating ourselves. So with this in mind, it seemed a natural step to include this kind of peek behind the scenes at what inspires me.

One of my fundamental fascinations with knitting is its meditative nature, so I was thrilled to see books being published that address this. Although meditation is a highly personal experience, when we are just learning, we are usually directed by prompts from an instructor, to focus on each breath, for example. So I devised each of the mindfulness pointers contained in the pattern instructions to mimic this process. In writing these, I drew upon comments made by my wonderful test knitters, as well as on my own personal experiences while working on projects contained here.

This book is not written for the brand-new knitter, but for those knitters who have acquired the basics and are now looking to build on these skills. It is also for the many "returning" knitters who have rekindled their love of the craft. Having the desire to take time to become more accomplished should be applauded! There can be joy in accepting a challenge and allowing yourself to reap the benefits of that journey. Without doing this, we cannot expect our craft to grow or evolve.

The inspirations behind the designs in this book are varied, and I have been open and honest about where they came from. My quirks are what give me my unique view of the world. Therefore, this book is a reflection of who I am right now, at this time, in this place.

In writing this book, I discovered that delving inward to observe, and then describe, how my designs develop has been a valuable tool on my path to self-discovery. I hope these patterns strike a chord with you, and that you enjoy hours of lovely con-templation as you knit them. I encourage you to harness the power of knitting as a tool for relaxation. But be aware that as you ponder and daydream, you can sometimes wander too far down the path of dreams and lose track of the pattern, so remain mindful while you create.

things you need to know before you begin

Cable knitting produces a raised, textured pattern that resembles twisted ropes. To achieve this look, groups of stitches are worked in an order different from how they present themselves on the left-hand (LH) needle. Cables are usually set on a fabric of reverse stockinette stitch (but not always) to highlight them.

Cables produce a raised surface and also contract the piece, producing a denser fabric. Therefore, more stitches and yarn are required to produce a particular width of cabled fabric than a fabric made using stockinette stitch.

how to work a cable

To change the order in which the stitches present themselves, a short, double-pointed needle (dpn), called a cable needle (CN), is used. Stitches are slipped from the LH needle onto one end of the cable needle and are worked off the other end.

THERE ARE THREE STEPS TO WORKING A CABLE:

1. Stitches are slipped from the LH needle onto the CN and held either at the back or at the front of the knitted piece.

2. Stitches are worked from the LH needle.

3. The stitches held on the CN are worked.

The result is stitches that appear to be crossed or twisted.

THERE ARE FOUR BASIC WAYS OF CROSSING OR TWISTING THE STITCHES:

1. Holding the stitches on the CN toward the back of the piece (away from you) as you work stitches from the LH needle; all stitches are knitted.

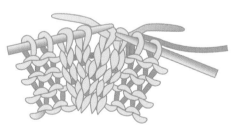

2. Holding the stitches on the CN toward the front of the piece (toward you) as you work stitches from the LH needle; all stitches are knitted.

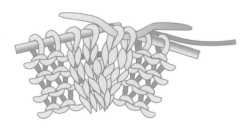

3. Holding the stitches on the CN toward the back of the piece, knitting the stitches from the LH needle, then purling the stitches from the cable needle.

4. Holding the stitches on the CN toward the front of the piece, purling the stitches from the LH needle, then knitting the stitches from the cable needle.

In addition to the four basic ways of creating a cable or twist, there are many variations, each of which produces a particular effect. Different cable patterns are achieved by varying the following:

· The number of stitches placed on the CN.

· The number of stitches worked from the LH needle.

· The order of knitting or purling stitches from the LH needle or CN.

· How often the crossing takes place, which changes the number of "rest" rows between each cross or twist.

· The combination of crosses or twists used to produce a pattern.

· The space (or lack of space) between the cable placements across the row.

TIPS FOR FOLLOWING CABLE INSTRUCTIONS

When the instruction abbreviation begins with a *C*, you will know that this is a cable, and that all stitches involved will be knitted. Whereas, when the instruction abbreviation begins with a *T*, you will know that this is a twist, and a combination of knit and purl stitches will be required.

When the instruction abbreviation ends with a *B*, you will know that the stitches slipped onto the CN will be held at the back while you work the stitches from the LH needle. When the instruction abbreviation ends with an *F*, you will know that the stitches slipped onto the CN will be held at the front while you are working the stitches from the LH needle.

The number included in an instruction such as C4B (cable 4 back) refers to the total number of stitches involved in creating the cable. So for C4B, the total number of stitches involved in the cable is four. When the number is an even one, it is usually divided in half. In other words, two stitches are slipped onto the CN and held at the back of the piece; then the next two stitches on the LH needle are knitted. To complete the cable, the two stitches on the CN are knitted. Similarly, for C6B (cable 6 back), a total of six stitches are involved. Three are held at the back on the CN while three stitches are knitted from the LH needle; then the three stitches on the CN are knitted.

When the instruction ends with an *R*, you know that the cable "cord" will appear to be moving across the fabric toward the right, and to the left if the instruction ends with an *L*.

Some instructions and symbols can look quite similar to each other. So please make sure that you read each instruction used in your chosen project carefully before you begin. Precise directions for each instruction can be found on the key to charts (page 15).

(page 15).

When selecting the size you wish to make, please refer to the schematic diagrams for your chosen project. These diagrams give the dimensions each instruction will produce when knitting at the gauge given for that project. I suggest that you measure a garment that you already have and like the fit of, then choose the size that is closest to it based on the schematic diagram.

GAUGE

This is very important! Please check your gauge carefully before you begin, by knitting a swatch. This will ensure that you achieve a desirable fabric and the correct size garment. To make a swatch, cast on enough stitches to be able to work at least a full repeat of the pattern indicated. This may mean that you will be working a swatch larger than 4 inches [10 cm x 10 cm] square. Once you have made and blocked your swatch, measure it in several places to confirm the gauge. If you have more stitches and rows than the instructions indicate, use larger needles (and rework the swatch). If you have fewer stitches and rows, use smaller needles (and rework the swatch).

CHARTS AND HOW TO READ THEM

Charts are used throughout the projects because I find them easier to follow than written instructions when working a detailed pattern. However, I know that this isn't true for everyone, so I have included written instructions, too.

I find charts easier to use because they are visual representations of the knitted fabric (viewed from the right side) in diagram form. Each square represents one stitch, and a line of squares represents one row.

Charts are followed beginning at the bottom and working toward the top, just as you knit. They are read from right to left for right side rows, then left to right for wrong side rows. The row number is given at the side where you will begin, to help you remember this. I suggest that you use a ruler or a piece of cardboard to slide along as you work, to help in reading row by row.

PATTERN REPEATS AND PLACING MARKERS

Pattern repeats are indicated by solid lines on the charts, and by an asterisk [*] in the written instructions. The number of stitches in a repeat is shown at the base of each chart. Use this when placing markers to indicate the placement of different cable patterns across a row. I suggest placing a marker at the beginning of each pattern repeat.

Using markers reduces the amount of stitch-counting you need to do and aids in trouble-shooting if you make a mistake. Some instructions will indicate the precise placement of markers for clarity, when shaping is occurring, for example. You may also chose to use markers in cases where not specifically called for.

Please note that in some projects the cable panels are worked one after the other. This may mean that a purl stitch, for example, may be followed by another purl stitch, producing a larger number of purls together; using markers will help to prevent any confusion.

Row counts for each repeat are shown up each side of the charts. Please note that in some projects—where multiple cables patterns are used, for example—the row counts may not coincide.

SLEEVE INCREASES

It is always a good idea to read through all the instructions for a pattern before you begin, but it is particularly important when working sleeves. Sometimes the instructions will give patterning details that need to be worked *at the same time* as increases.

FINISHING

I highly recommend blocking all pieces before you begin to join each project. To do this, lay each piece out on a flat, padded surface and pin out to the dimensions given in the schematic diagram. Then place a damp cloth over the piece and either leave until completely dry, or hold an iron just above the cloth, moving it in an up-and-down motion (not side to side), letting steam penetrate the fabric. Do not press down on the piece, to avoid crushing the raised cables. Leave until completely cool and dry. Consult the yarn label for care information; yarns containing synthetic fibers should not be ironed.

There are many methods for joining seams, so I suggest consulting your knitting reference book when selecting which one to use. In most instances in this book, the mattress stitch was used, unless where a specific method has been indicated.

SETTING IN SLEEVES

Fold the sleeve in half and place a marker to indicate the center point at the top of sleeve cap. Pin the sleeve into the armhole, matching your marker to the shoulder seam. Match any bound-off stitches at the beginning of the cap shaping to bound-off stitches at the beginning of armhole shaping on the body pieces. Then ease the remaining fabric into the armhole between these points and pin in place. Stitch in place. Remove the pins.

techniques

The following explanations are for the methods and techniques used in the pattern instructions.

BACK STITCH: Beginning approximately $1/4$ in [5 mm] from lower/upper edge, take needle down through work to the WS of work at the lower/upper edge. *Bring needle back through to the RS approx $1/4$ in [5 mm] ahead of original starting point. Pull up thread. Take needle back through to WS again at the starting point for previous stitch. Repeat from * to end.

FAIR ISLE TECHNIQUE: This technique is used when two colors are worked in the same row. To avoid having long floats on the WS of the fabric and causing the fabric to pucker, carry the unused color over a maximum of three stitches. If the unused color will be required to be carried over more than three stitches, gently twist yarns around each other after three stitches have been worked; then continue with yarn already being used.

I-CORDS: I-cords are made using a pair of double-pointed needles (dpns). Cast on the required number of stitches and knit them. *Do not turn the needle. Simply slide the stitches to the opposite end of needle, pull the yarn across the back of the stitches,

and knit them once more.* Repeat from * to * until desired length.

A strand will be produced on the wrong side (WS), but as you work, you will see that each end of the rows will curl toward each other to form a tube and enclose this strand.

SHORT ROWS: Short row shaping is used for shoulder shaping, rather than the usual binding off stitches. As you work across the row, the instructions will tell you to work a certain number of stitches. Wrap the next stitch, which prevents a hole from forming. Then turn the work, leaving the remaining stitches unworked, which are described as being "held."

To wrap a stitch: work to turn point; with yarn in back, slip the next stitch purlwise to the right-hand (RH) needle; bring yarn to front and then slip the same stitch back onto the LH needle. Turn work and bring yarn into position for next stitch, wrapping the stitch as you do. When you work across all the stitches once again, it is necessary to pick up the wraps to prevent them from showing on the right side (RS) of the fabric.

Picking up wraps: work to the stitch that is wrapped; insert tip of RH needle from the front under the wrap from bottom up and then into the wrapped stitch

as usual. Knit them together, making sure the new stitch comes out under the wrap.

3-NEEDLE BIND OFF: This technique is used for joining seams by knitting them together rather than sewing them. It can be used decoratively, worked on the RS of the garment, using a contrast color.

Begin by having each set of stitches that are to be joined on separate needles. Place garment pieces together as indicated in instructions; right sides together will produce a seam on the inside of the garment, wrong sides together will produce a seam visible on the outside of the garment. Both needles need to be pointing in the same direction at this point.

Using a third needle, knit the first stitch from one needle together with the first stitch from the second needle, * knit next stitch from each needle together, bind off first stitch on right needle in the usual manner. Repeat from * to end.

WHIP STITCH: Bring needle from the back to the front. *Take needle across at a right angle, approximately $1/4$ in [5 mm] away, and through to the back. Then bring needle through to the front once more directly above end point of last stitch. Pull up thread. Repeat from * to end.

glossary

GARTER RIDGE: 2 or more knit rows following stockinette stitch or reverse stockinette stitch.

GARTER STITCH: Knit all rows.

REVERSE STOCKINETTE STITCH: Purl right side rows; knit wrong side rows, (reverse of stockinette stitch).

SEED STITCH: When worked over an odd number of stitches, row 1: (k1, p1) to last stitch, end k1. Row 2: repeat row 1. When worked over an even number of stitches, row 1: (k1, p1) to end. Row 2: (p1, k1) to end.

STOCKINETTE STITCH: Knit on right-side rows; purl on wrong-side rows.

WORK EVEN: Continue working without increasing or decreasing stitches.

needle conversion chart

METRIC	U.S. SIZES	CANADIAN/ U.K. SIZES
10	15	000
9	13	00
8	11	0
7.5	—	1
7	—	2
6.5	10.5	3
6	10	4
5.5	9	5
5	8	6
4.5	7	7
4	6	8
3.75	5	9
3.5	4	—
3.25	3	10
3	—	11
2.75	2	12
2.25	1	13
2	0	14
1.75	—	15

abbreviations

ALT: alternate

APPROX: approximate(ly)

BEG: beginning

BO: bind off

C: cable

CB: center back

CF: center front

CM: centimeters

CN: cable needle

COLOR A, B, ETC.: indicates contrast colors

CONT: continue(ing)

DEC: decrease

DPN: double-pointed needle

FOLL: following

IN: inch(es)

INC: increase

INC 2: increase 2 stitches by working k1, p1, k1 all into next stitch

K: knit

K2TOG: knit 2 stitches together

K2TOGB: knit 2 stitches together through back of loops

LH: left-hand (as in "left-hand needle")

LHS: left-hand side

M1: make 1 stitch by picking up the strand between the next 2 stitches

M/C: main color

P: purl

PB: purl through back of loop

P2TOG: purl 2 stitches together

P2TOGB: purl 2 stitches together through back of loop

P3TOG: purl 3 stitches together

PATT(S): pattern(s)

PSSO: pass slipped stitch over

REM: remaining

REP: repeat

REV ST ST: reverse stockinette stitch, purl on right side rows, knit on wrong side rows

RH: right-hand (as in "right-hand needle")

RHS: right-hand side

RND(S): round(s)

RS: right side

SL: slip

SL2KNITWISE-K1-P2SSO: slip 2 stitches together as if to knit, knit next stitch from LH needle, pass both slipped stitches together over knitted stitch

SSK: slip next 2 stitches one at a time knitwise onto right needle; then knit them together in that position using left needle and working through front of loops

ST(S): stitch(es)

ST ST: stockinette stitch, knit on right side rows, purl on wrong side rows

T: twist

TBL: through back of loop

TOG: together

WS: wrong side

YB: yarn back

YFON: bring yarn forward and over needle

YFWD: yarn forward

YO: yarn over

YRN: yarn

*: designates the starting point for a repetition of a series of instructions

( ): alternative measurements or instructions

Key to Charts

☐	k on RS; p on WS	⊡	p on RS; k on WS
◼	no stitch	⧄	k2tog
Ⓜ	inc2	⧄	p3tog
Ⓜ	inc4	⧄	dec4
m	make 1		

☐ PB   Purl through back of loop on WS rows

⧅ ssk   Slip next 2 sts knitwise, one at a time; then knit them tog through front of loops from the left

⃞ yfon   Bring yarn to front and allow it to wrap over needle as you work next st

C2B   Slip next st onto CN & hold at back; k1 from LH needle; then k1 from CN

C2F   Slip next st onto CN & hold at front; k1 from LH needle; then k1 from CN

T2B   Slip next st onto CN & hold at back; k1 from LH needle; then p1 from CN

T2F   Slip next st onto CN & hold at front; p1 from LH needle; then k1 from CN

C2BW   (worked on WS row): slip next st onto CN; hold at back; p1 from LH needle; then p1 from CN

C2FW   (worked on WS row): slip next st onto CN; hold at front, p1 from LH needle; then p1 from CN

C3B   Slip next st onto CN & hold at back; k2 from LH needle; then k1 from CN

C3F   Slip next 2 sts onto CN & hold at front, k1 from LH needle; then k2 from CN

T3B   Slip next st onto CN & hold at back, k2 from LH needle; then p1 from CN

T3F   Slip next 2 sts onto CN & hold at front, p1 from LH needle; then k2 from CN

C4B   Slip next 2 sts onto CN & hold at back, k2 from LH needle; then k2 from CN

C4F   Slip next 2 sts onto CN & hold at front, k2 from LH needle; then k2 from CN

T4B   Slip next 2 sts onto CN & hold at back, k2 from LH needle; then p2 from CN

T4F   Slip next 2 sts onto CN & hold at front, p2 from LH needle; then k2 from CN

T4R   Slip next st onto CN & hold at back, k3 from LH needle; then p1 from CN

T4L   Slip next 3 sts onto CN, hold at front, p1 from LH needle; then k3 from CN

C5B   Slip next 2 sts onto CN & hold at back, k3 from LH needle; then k2 from CN

C5F   Slip next 3 sts onto CN & hold at front, k2 from LH needle; then k3 from CN

T5R   Slip next 2 sts onto CN & hold at back, k3 from LH needle; then p2 from CN

T5L   Slip next 3 sts onto CN & hold at front, p2 from LH needle; then k3 from CN

T5BP   Slip next 3 sts onto CN & hold at back of work, k2 from LH needle; then p1, k2 from CN

C6B   Slip next 3 sts onto CN, hold at back, k3 from LH needle; then k3 from CN

C6F   Slip next 3 sts onto CN, hold at front, k3 from LH needle; then k3 from CN

T6B   Slip next 3 sts onto CN, hold at back, k3 from LH needle; then p3 from CN

T6F   Slip next 3 sts onto CN, hold at front, p3 from LH needle; then k3 from CN

T6Rrib   Twist 6 right rib; slip next 4 sts onto CN & hold at back of work, knit next 2 sts from LH needle, slip the 2 purl sts from CN back onto LH needle and purl them, k2 from CN

T6Lrib   Twist 6 left rib; slip next 4 sts onto CN & hold at front of work, knit next 2 sts from LH needle, slip the 2 purl sts from CN back onto LH needle and purl them, k2 from CN

inspired by change

CABLE PATTERNS DON'T HAVE TO BE STRICTLY VERT-
ICAL IN PLACEMENT, AS TRADITION WOULD HAVE US
BELIEVE. THEY CAN CHANGE OR "MORPH" INTO NEW ALIGNMENTS
SO THAT THEY APPEAR TO DETERMINE THEIR OWN PATHS THROUGH
THE GARMENT PIECE.

Most traditional cable-knit patterns place the cables vertically, with
the repetition of rows continuing until you reach the neckline, where
you simply bind off and then start the same thing all over again for the
next piece. Sometimes, cables are placed horizontally or diagonally, and
might even appear to wander back and forth, but the repetition of a
pattern is still present. But what if we escape from the repetition?

I believe that what causes most of us to stall in completing a project is
the repetition of the same few rows, over and over. It's fun at first, but
once we learn the pattern, we need something else to keep us interested,
a carrot dangled before us. What most of us do when we feel we are in a
rut is to make a change.

The power of change is remarkable. The excitement of new things—a
new home, friend, or even a piece of music—affects us deeply. I created
the following designs to illustrate my fascination with transformation
and to offer knitters new possibilities in cable knitting.

joining in friendship

Friendships develop from fragments of time two people spend together, some long and lingering, some short and snatched. But all are necessary to build a friendship.

When we unexpectedly bump into a friend, it brightens our day, makes us smile, and adds a little detail to the friendship. Similarly, each stitch builds on the one that came before, becoming first a row, and eventually a whole sweater.

What if cables were also to mirror our life experiences? Our lives are not straight paths moving ahead without interruption. We are changed by life events and the relationships we form. To reflect this, the familiar, repetitive vertical cables would also need to change.

In this pattern, one cable meanders to and fro, mirroring the path of an adventurous friend; the other cable is on a different path, coming and going at intervals while managing to remain steady and true, something to depend on. The cables link together at the yoke, the heart center, to form a new, more uniform pattern, as two individuals do when they join together in friendship.

SIZES / FINISHED CHEST MEASUREMENTS

Small 35 in [89 cm]
Medium 38 in [96.5 cm]
Large 42 in [106.5 cm]
XL 46 in [117 cm]
2X 50 in [127 cm]

Instructions are given for the smallest size. If changes are necessary for larger sizes, the instructions are given in ( ). Where there is only one set of figures, this applies to all sizes.

MATERIALS

Alpaca/Merino by Sweaterkits, shade Cranberry, 11 (11-12-13-14) 50 g balls (40% alpaca–60% merino).

Pair of 4 mm needles, 6 stitch holders, CN.

Yarn amounts given are based on average requirements and are approximate.

TENSION / GAUGE

25 sts and 30 rows = 4 in [10 cm] over cable pattern.

Take the time to check your gauge; change needle sizes if necessary to obtain correct gauge and garment size.

REFER TO THE GLOSSARY ON PAGE 13 FOR: SEED STITCH, AND TO TECHNIQUES ON PAGE 12 FOR: 3-NEEDLE BIND OFF AND SHORT ROWS.

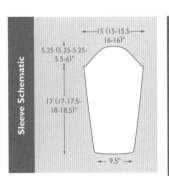

Sleeve Schematic

15 (15-15.5-16-16)"
5.25 (5.25-5.25-5.5-6)"
17 (17-17.5-18-18.5)"
9.5"

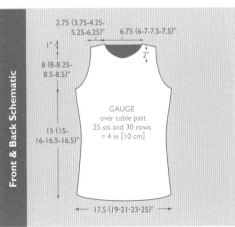

Front & Back Schematic

2.75 (3.75-4.25-5.25-6.25)"   6.75 (6-7-7.5-7.5)"
1"
2"
8 (8-8.25-8.5-8.5)"
GAUGE
over cable patt
25 sts and 30 rows
= 4 in [10 cm]
15 (15-16-16.5-16.5)"
17.5 (19-21-23-25)"

Symbols Used in These Charts

- ⊡ p on RS; k on WS
- ☐ k on RS; p on WS
- ◩ ssk
- ☑ k2tog
- �🅼 make 1
- T3B
- T3F
- C3B
- C3F
- C4B
- C4F

Chart A

Chart reads R to L RS rows
and L to R WS rows

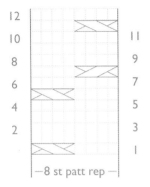

—8 st patt rep—

Chart C

Chart reads R to L RS rows and L to R WS rows

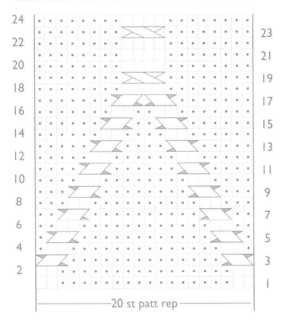

—20 st patt rep—

Chart B

Chart reads R to L RS rows and L to R WS rows

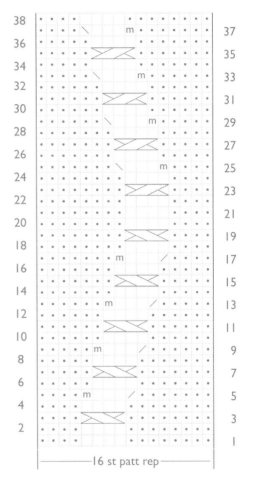

—16 st patt rep—

Chart D

Chart reads R to L RS rows and L to R WS rows

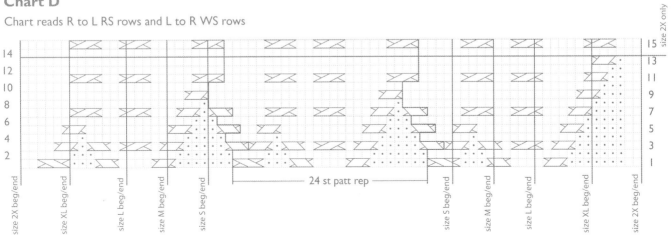

—24 st patt rep—

size 2X beg/end
size XL beg/end
size L beg/end
size M beg/end
size S beg/end
size S beg/end
size M beg/end
size L beg/end
size XL beg/end
size 2X beg/end

size 2X only

Note: avoid working partial cables; replace at beginnings and ends of rows with knit stitches.

PATTERN A

Row 1 (RS): k4, C4F.

Row 2 and all WS rows: p8.

Row 3: k8.

Rows 5 and 6: rep rows 1 and 2.

Row 7: C4B, k4.

Row 9: as row 3.

Row 11: as row 7.

Row 12: p8.

Rep rows 1–12 for patt A.

PATTERN B

Row 1 (RS): p8, k4, p4.

Row 2: k4, p4, k8.

Row 3: p8, C4F, p4.

Row 4: rep row 2.

Row 5: p7, k2tog, k3, m1, p4.

Row 6: k5, p4, k7.

Row 7: p7, C4F, p5.

Row 8: rep row 6.

Row 9: p6, k2tog, k3, m1, p5.

Row 10: k6, p4, k6.

Row 11: p6, C4F, p6.

Row 12: rep row 10.

Row 13: p5, k2tog, k3, m1, p6.

Row 14: k7, p4, k5.

Row 15: p5, C4F, p7.

Row 16: rep row 14.

Row 17: p4, k2tog, k3, m1, p7.

Row 18: k8, p4, k4.

Row 19: p4, C4F, p8.

Row 20: rep row 18.

Row 21: p4, k4, p8.

Row 22: rep row 18.

Row 23: p4, C4B, p8.

Row 24: rep row 18.

Row 25: p4, m1, k3, ssk, p7.

Row 26: rep row 14.

Row 27: p5, C4B, p7.

Row 28: rep row 14.

Row 29: p5, m1, k3, ssk, p6.

Row 30: rep row 10.

Row 31: p6, C4B, p6.

Row 32: rep row 10.

Row 33: p6, m1, k3, ssk, p5.

Row 34: rep row 6.

Row 35: p7, C4B, p5.

Row 36: rep row 6.

Row 37: p7, m1, k3, ssk, p4.

Row 38: rep row 2.

Rep rows 1–38 for patt B.

PATTERN C

Row 1 (RS): k2, p16, k2.

Row 2: p2, k16, p2.

Row 3: T3F, p14, T3B.

Row 4: k1, p2, k14, p2, k1.

Row 5: p1, T3F, p12, T3B, p1.

Row 6: k2, p2, k12, p2, k2.

Row 7: p2, T3F, p10, T3B, p2.

Row 8: k3, p2, k10, p2, k3.

Row 9: p3, T3F, p8, T3B, p3.

Row 10: k4, p2, k8, p2, k4.

Row 11: p4, T3F, p6, T3B, p4.

Row 12: k5, p2, k6, p2, k5.

Row 13: p5, T3F, p4, T3B, p5.

Row 14: k6, p2, k4, p2, k6.

Row 15: p6, T3F, p2, T3B, p6.

Row 16: k7, p2, k2, p2, k7.

Row 17: p7, T3F, T3B, p7.

Row 18: k8, p4, k8.

Row 19: p8, C4F, p8.

Row 20: rep row 18.

Row 21: p8, k4, p8.

Row 22: rep row 18.

Rows 23 and 24: rep rows 19 and 20.

BACK

Using 4 mm needles, cast on 110 (120-130-144-156) sts.

Work 2 rows in seed st, then place cable panels as follows:

RS set up row: p3 (8-13-20-26), (k8, work 16 st patt rep row 1 Chart B) 4 times, k8, p3 (8-13-20-26).

WS set up row: k3 (8-13-20-26), (p8, work 16 st patt rep row 2 Chart B) 4 times, p8, k3 (8-13-20-26).

Row 1 (RS): p3 (8-13-20-26), (work 8 st patt row 1 Chart A, then 16 st patt rep row 3 Chart B) 4 times, then work 8 st patt rep row 1 Chart A once more, p3 (8-13-20-26).

Row 2: k3 (8-13-20-26), (work 8 st patt rep row 2 Chart A, then 16 st patt rep row 4 Chart B) 4 times, then work 8 st patt rep row 2 Chart A once more, k3 (8-13-20-26).

Cont working chart rows in sequence as set until piece measures 4.5 (3.5-4-4.25-4.25) in [11.5 (9-10-10.75-10.75) cm] from beg, end with RS row facing for next row.

shape waist as follows:

Cont in patt, dec 1 st at each end of next row, work 7 rows even in patt. Rep last 8 rows 1 (2-2-2-2) more times, then work dec row once again, 104 (112-122-136-148) sts rem. Work 11 rows even in patt. Cont in patt inc 1 st at each end of next row, work 7 rows even in patt. Rep last 8 rows 1 (2-2-2-2) more times, then inc row again, 110 (120-130-144-156) sts.

Cont working even in patt until piece measures approx 15 (15-16-16.5-16.5) in [38 (38-40.5-42-42) cm] from beg, end working row 34 (34-4-6-6) of Chart B.

shape armholes as follows:

Cont in patt, BO 6 sts at beg of next 2 rows. Dec 1 st at each end of next 6 rows, then dec 1 st at each end of RS rows 4 times, 78 (88-98-112-124) sts rem. Work even until piece measures approx 3.5 (3.5-2.5-2-2) in [9 (9-6.5-5-5) cm] from beg of armhole shaping, end working row 22 of Chart B.

yoke transition:

Work following rows 1–13 of Chart D for sizes S, M, L, and XL. Work following rows 1–15 Chart D for size 2X. Beg and end each row where indicated for size, working 24 st patt rep 3 times.***

Cont rep rows 10–13 Chart D for sizes S, M, L, and XL, and rows 12–15 Chart D for size 2X, until armhole measures 8 (8-8.25-8.5-8.5) in [20 (20-21-21.5-21.5) cm] from beg of shaping, end RS row facing for next row.

shape shoulders as follows:

Cont in patt as now set,

Next row: work to last 6 (8-9-11-13) sts, wrap next st, turn, leave rem sts unworked in hold. WS row: rep last row.

Next row: work to last 12 (16-18-22-26) sts, wrap next st, turn. Rep this row.

Next row: work to last 18 (24-27-33-39) sts, wrap next st, turn. Rep this row.

Place each set of sts for shoulders onto separate stitch holders and

center 42 (40-44-46-46) sts onto another stitch holder for back neck.

FRONT

Work as given for back to ***.

Cont rep rows 10–13 Chart D for sizes S, M, L, and XL, and rows 12–15 Chart D for size 2X, until armhole measures 6 (6-6.25-6.5-6.5) in [15 (15-16-16.5-16.5) cm] from beg of shaping, end with RS row facing for next row.

shape front neck as follows:

Work across 33 (39-42-48-54) sts in patt, turn (this is neck edge). Leave rem 45 (49-56-64-70) sts on a spare needle. Cont in patt, dec 1 st at neck edge on next 15 rows, 18 (24-27-33-39) sts rem. Work even until piece measures the same as back before shoulder shaping, end WS row facing for next row.

shape shoulder as follows:

Work to last 6 (8-9-11-13) sts, wrap next st, turn, leave rem sts unworked in hold. Work RS row even.

Next row: work to last 12 (16-18-22-26) sts, wrap next st, turn. Work RS row even. Place 18 (24-27-33-39) sts for shoulder onto stitch holder.

Return to sts on spare needle. Slip center 12 (10-14-16-16) sts onto a stitch holder, rejoin yarn to rem 33 (39-42-48-54) sts and work to end in patt. Dec 1 st at neck edge on next 15 rows, 18 (24-27-33-39) sts rem. Work even until piece measures the same as back before shoulder shaping, end with RS row facing for next row.

shape shoulder as follows:
Work to last 6 (8-9-11-13) sts, wrap next st, turn, leave rem sts unworked in hold. Work WS row even.

Next row: work to last 12 (16-18-22-26) sts, wrap next st, turn. Work WS row even. Place 18 (24-27-33-39) sts for shoulder onto stitch holder.

SLEEVE (MAKE 2 ALIKE)

With 4 mm needles, cast on 60 sts, work 2 rows in seed st, then place cable as follows:

Row 1 (RS): (work 20 st patt rep row 1 Chart C) 3 times.

Row 2: (work 20 st patt rep row 2 Chart C) 3 times.

Cont working Chart C rows in sequence as set, *at the same time* inc 1 st at each end of chart rows 7, 15 and 23, work inc sts in rev St St throughout, 66 sts.

Now place Chart B as follows:

RS: p3, (work 16 st patt rep row 1 Chart B, p4) twice, then work 16 st patt rep row 1 Chart B once more, p7.

WS: k7, (work 16 st patt rep row 2 Chart B, k4) twice, then work 16 st patt rep row 2 Chart B once more, k3.

Cont working Chart B rows in sequence, *at the same time* inc 1 st at each end of row 7 of chart and every following 8th row 8 (8-6-4-4) times, 84 (84-80-76-76) sts. Then inc 1 st at each end of every following 6th row 4 (4-7-11-11) times, 92 (92-94-98-98) sts. Work even in patt until sleeve measures 17 (17-17.5-18-18.5) in [43 (43-44.5-45.75-47) cm], end with RS row facing for next row.

shape cap as follows:
Cont in patt, BO 4 sts at beg of next 2 rows. Dec 1 st at each end of following 10 (10-10-11-12) RS rows, 64 (64-66-68-66) sts rem. Then dec 1 st at each end of every row 14 times, 36 (36-38-40-38) sts rem. BO 4 (4-5-5-5) sts at beg of next 4 rows. BO rem 20 (20-18-20-18) sts.

Weave in ends. Block pieces to given dimensions.

Join RHS shoulder seam using 3-needle bind-off method.

Beg at LHS shoulder with RS facing, using 4 mm needle pick up and knit 19 (21-20-21-21) sts down LHS front neck, knit across 12 (10-14-16-16) sts from front st holder, then pick up and knit 19 (21-20-21-21) sts up RHS front neck, then knit across 42 (40-44-46-46) sts from back st holder, inc 1 st at CB, 93 (93-99-105-105) sts total. Work back and forth as follows:

WS row: (k3, p3) to last 3 sts, k3.

RS row: (p3, k3) to last 3 sts, p3. Rep these 2 rows until turtleneck measures 6 in [15 cm]. BO in rib as set.

Join LHS shoulder using 3-needle BO method. Sew turtleneck seam. Set in sleeves to armholes. Sew side and sleeve seams.

Press lightly, following the instructions on the yarn label.

mindfulness pointer: the comfort of friendship

My knitter, Joan, worked on this project in stops and starts. She described the feeling of returning to the cables each time as reminiscent of reuniting with an old friend; her hands remembered the stitches and brought the comfort of familiarity along with them.

We have all experienced a project that we began with great excitement only to later put aside because something else came along. As you start this project, resolve to spend time with your "friend," even if it is just for a few rows a day. Those stolen moments eventually add up, becoming more than the sum of their parts. Each day, remind yourself that the comfort of friendship is right there waiting for you—just pick up the needles!

go with the flow

One of the great debates in life is the notion of free will versus that of predestination, or fate. It is a topic that I love to discuss, and I could do so late into the night. I am open to both schools of thought and have yet to make a firm decision about which side I favor.

I do believe, however, that it is up to each of us to choose how we will respond to what life throws our way. To feel contented, we must try to fully accept the obstacles as well as the opportunites that life presents—to accept the good along with the bad. I try to live by the mantra "go with the flow" as much as possible.

I based the design for this tank on that mantra. I selected elements that had a yielding rather than a dogmatic, set-in-stone quality. The lace pattern produces a waved edging rather than a hard, blunt, cast-on edge, while the soft, undulating cables flow out and back from the stockinette-stitch side panels. Then, in the center of the panel, the cables intertwine as though acknowledging their neighbors, willing to embrace a new element. As the pattern reaches the neckline, it flows gently around its curve.

SIZES / FINISHED CHEST MEASUREMENTS

X-Small 33 in [84 cm]
Small 36 in [91.5 cm]
Medium 38 in [96.5 cm]
Large 40 in [101.5 cm]
XL 42 in [106.5 cm]

Instructions are given for smallest size. If changes are necessary for larger sizes, instructions are given in ( ). Where there is only one set of figures, this applies to all sizes.

MATERIALS

Stork by Dale of Norway, shade 7, 4 (4-5-5-6) 50 g balls (100% Egyptian Cotton).

Pair of 2.5 mm needles, 2 stitch holders, CN.

Yarn amounts given are based on average requirements and are approximate.

TENSION / GAUGE

29 sts and 40 rows = 4 in [10 cm] over stocking stitch.

Take the time to check your gauge; change needle sizes if necessary to obtain correct gauge and garment size.

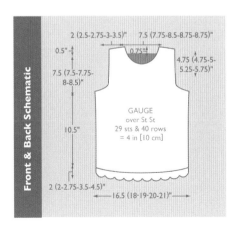

Front & Back Schematic

2 (2.5-2.75-3-3.5)"   7.5 (7.75-8.5-8.75-8.75)"
0.5"   0.75"
7.5 (7.5-7.75-8-8.5)"   4.75 (4.75-5-5.25-5.75)"
10.5"
GAUGE
over St St
29 sts & 40 rows
= 4 in [10 cm]
2 (2-2.75-3.5-4.5)"
16.5 (18-19-20-21)"

Symbols Used in These Charts

⊡	p on RS; k on WS	⧗	C2B		T3B		C4B		T4R		C5B
☐	k on RS; p on WS				T3F		C4F		T4L		C5F
							T4B				T5R
							T4F				T5L
											T5BP

Chart A

Chart reads R to L RS rows and L to R WS rows

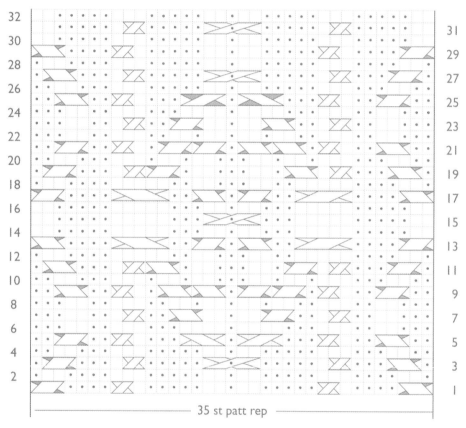

35 st patt rep

Chart B

Chart reads R to L RS rows and L to R WS rows

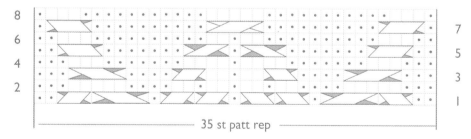

35 st patt rep

PATTERN A
(CABLE PANEL)

Row 1 (RS): T3F, p4, k1, C2B, p5, k2, p1, k2, p5, k1, C2B, p4, T3B.

Row 2: k1, p2, k4, p3, k5, p2, k1, p2, k5, p3, k4, p2, k1.

Row 3: p1, T3F, p3, C2B, k1, p5, T5BP, p5, C2B, k1, p3, T3B, p1.

Row 4: k2, p2, k3, p3, k5, p2, k1, p2, k5, p3, k3, p2, k2.

Row 5: p2, T3F, p2, k1, C2B, p3, C4B, p1, C4F, p3, k1, C2B, p2, T3B, p2.

Row 6: k3, p2, k2, p3, k3, p4, k1, p4, k3, p3, k2, p2, k3.

Row 7: p3, k2, p2, C2B, k1, p2, T3B, k2, p1, k2, T3F, p2, C2B, k1, p2, k2, p3.

Row 8: k3, p2, k2, p3, k2, (p2, k1) 3 times, p2, k2, p3, k2, p2, k3.

Row 9: p2, T3B, p2, k1, C2B, p1, (T3B) twice, p1, (T3F) twice, p1, k1, C2B, p2, T3F, p2.

Row 10: k2, p2, k3, p3, (k1, p2) twice, k3, (p2, k1) twice, p3, k3, p2, k2.

Row 11: p1, T3B, p3, C2B, k1, T3B, p1, k2, p3, k2, p1, T3F, C2B, k1, p3, T3F, p1.

Row 12: k1, p2, k4, p5, k2, p2, k3, p2, k2, p5, k4, p2, k1.

Row 13: T3B, p4, C5B, p2, T3F, p1, T3B, p2, C5F, p4, T3F.

Row 14: p2, k5, p5, k3, p2, k1, p2, k3, p5, k5, p2.

Row 15: k2, p5, k5, p3, T5BP, p3, k5, p5, k2.

Row 16: rep row 14.

Row 17: T3F, p4, C5B, p2, T3B, p1, T3F, p2, C5F, p4, T3B.

Row 18: rep row 12.

Row 19: p1, T3F, p3, C2B, k1, T3F, p1, k2, p3, k2, p1, T3B, C2B, k1, p3, T3B, p1.

Row 20: rep row 10.

Row 21: p2, T3F, p2, k1, C2B, p1, (T3F) twice, p1, (T3B) twice, p1, k1, C2B, p2, T3B, p2.

Row 22: rep row 8.

Row 23: p3, k2, p2, C2B, k1, p2, T3F, k2, p1, k2, T3B, p2, C2B, k1, p2, k2, p3.

Row 24: rep row 6.

Row 25: p2, T3B, p2, k1, C2B, p3, T4F, p1, T4B, p3, k1, C2B, p2, T3F, p2.

Row 26: rep row 4.

Row 27: p1, T3B, p3, C2B, k1, p5, T5BP, p5, C2B, k1, p3, T3F, p1.

Row 28: rep row 2.

Row 29: T3B, p4, k1, C2B, p5, k2, p1, k2, p5, k1, C2B, p4, T3F.

Row 30: p2, k5, p3, k5, p2, k1, p2, k5, p3, k5, p2.

Row 31: k2, p5, C2B, k1, p5, T5BP, p5, C2B, k1, p5, k2.

Row 32: rep row 30.

Rep rows 1–32 for patt.

PATTERN B
(TRANSITION)

Row 1 (RS): p2, T3F, T5R, p1, (T3F) twice, p1, (T3B) twice, p1, T5L, T3B, p2.

Row 2: k3, p5, k4, (p2, k1) 3 times, p2, k4, p5, k3.

Row 3: p3, T5R, p4, T3F, k2, p1, k2, T3B, p4, T5L, p3.

Row 4: k3, p3, k7, p4, k1, p4, k7, p3, k3.

Row 5: p2, T4R, p7, T4F, p1, T4B, p7, T4L, p2.

Row 6: k2, p3, k10, p2, k1, p2, k10, p3, k2.

Row 7: p1, T4R, p10, C5B, p10, T4L, p1.

Row 8: k1, p3, k11, p5, k11, p3, k1.

BACK

Using 2.5 mm needles, cast on 123 (143-143-163-163) sts, knit 1 row.

eyelet row:

k1, (yo, k2tog) to end. Purl 1 row.

work scalloped edge as follows:

Row 1 (RS): k1, C2B, *(k1, yo) 3 times, (ssk) twice, sl2 knitwise-k1-p2sso, (k2tog) twice, (yo, k1) 3 times, k1, C2B, rep from * to end.

Row 2: purl.

Row 3: C2B, k1, *(k1, yo) 3 times, (ssk) twice, sl2 knitwise-k1-p2sso, (k2tog) twice, (yo, k1) 3 times, C2B, k1, rep from * to end.

Row 4: purl.

Rep these 4 rows once more.

lace stitch:

Row 1 (RS): k1, C2B, *k1, yo, ssk, k1, k2tog, yo, k5, yo, ssk, k1, k2tog, yo, k2, C2B, rep from * to end.

Row 2 and all WS rows: purl.

Row 3: C2B, *k2, yo, k1, sl1-k2tog-psso, k1, yo, k5, yo, k1, sl1-k2tog-psso, k1, yo, k1, C2B, rep from * to last st, k1.

Row 5: k1, C2B, *k1, k2tog, yo, k1, yo, ssk, k5, k2tog, yo, k1, yo, ssk, k2, C2B, rep from * to end.

Row 7: C2B, *k1, k2tog, (k1, yo) twice, k1, sl1-k1-psso, k3, k2tog, (k1, yo) twice, k1, sl1-k1-psso, C2B, rep from * to last st, k1.

Row 8: purl.

Rep previous 8 rows 1 (1-2-3-4) more times, then repeat rows 1 and 2 once again, dec 0 (10-2-16-8) sts across last row as follows:

XS: no dec, 123 sts rem.

S: (p8, p2tog) 5 times, p43, (p2tog, p8) 5 times, 133 sts rem.

M: p48, p2tog, p43, p2tog, p48, 141 sts rem.

L: (p6, p2tog) 8 times, p35, (p2tog, p6) 8 times, 147 sts rem.

XL: (p13, p2tog) 4 times, p43, (p2tog, p13) 4 times, 155 sts rem.

work center cable panel set-up rows as follows:
RS row: k45 (50-54-57-61), p5, C2B, k1, p4, p2tog, k2, p1, k2, p2tog, p4, C2B, k1, p5, knit to end, 121 (131-139-145-153) sts rem.

WS row: p45 (50-54-57-61), k5, p3, k5, p2, k1, p2, k5, p3, k5, purl to end.

Now place center panel as follows:

Row 1: k43 (48-52-55-59), work row 1 of Chart A, knit to end.

Row 2: p43 (48-52-55-59), work row 2 of Chart A, purl to end.

Cont working Chart A rows in sequence as set until piece measures approx 12.5 (12.5-13.25-14-15) in [32 (32-33.5-35.5-38) cm] at side seam edge, end row 1 of chart facing for next row.

shape armholes as follows:
Cont with center panel as set, BO 6 sts at beg of next 2 rows and 3 sts at beg of next 4 rows. Then dec 1 st at each end of following 7 RS rows, 83 (93-101-107-115) sts rem.

Work WS row even, row 20 of chart completed. ***

Cont even in patt until armhole measures 6.75 (6.75-7-7.25-7.75) in [17(17-18-18.5-19.5) cm] from beg of shaping, end with RS row facing for next row.

shape back neck as follows:
Cont in patt, work across 18 (22-24-26-30) sts, turn (this is neck edge). Leave rem 65 (71-77-81-85) sts on a spare needle.

Dec 1 st at neck edge on next 4 rows, 14 (18-20-22-26) sts. Work WS row even in patt.

shape shoulder as follows:
BO 5 (6-7-7-9) sts at beg of next row. Work WS row even. Rep last 2 rows once more. BO rem 4 (6-6-8-8) sts.

Return to sts on spare needle. Slip center 47 (49-53-55-55) sts

onto a stitch holder. Rejoin yarn to rem 18 (22-24-26-30) sts and work in patt to end. Dec 1 st at neck edge on next 4 rows, 14 (18-20-22-26) sts rem. Work 2 rows even in patt.

shape shoulder as follows:
BO 5 (6-7-7-9) sts at beg of next row. Work RS row even. Rep last 2 rows once more. BO rem 4 (6-6-8-8) sts.

FRONT

Work as given for back until completion of armhole shaping, marked ***.

Cont even working rows 1–8 given for transition patt Chart B placed over previous chart.

shape front neck (LHS) as follows:
RS row: k22 (27-31-34-38), k2tog, p1, k3, p6, turn (this is neck edge). Leave rem 49 (54-58-61-65) sts on a spare needle.

WS row: BO 2 sts at beg of row, knit 3 more sts (4 sts on RH needle), p3, k1, p to end.

RS row: k21 (26-30-33-37), k2tog, p1, k3, p4.

WS row: BO 2 sts at beg of row, knit 1 more st (2 sts on RH needle), p3, k1, p to end.

RS row: k20 (25-29-32-36), k2tog, p1, k3, p2, 27 (32-36-39-43) sts rem.

WS row: k2, p3, k1, purl to end.

RS row: knit to last 8 sts, k2tog, p1, k3, p2.

Rep the last 2 rows 12 (13-15-16-16) more times, 14 (18-20-22-26) sts rem.

WS row: k2, p3, k1, purl to end.

RS row: knit to last 6 sts, p1, k3, p2.

Rep last 2 rows until armhole measures the same as back before shoulder shaping, end with RS row facing for next row.

shape shoulder as follows:
BO 5 (6-7-7-9) sts at beg of next row. Work WS row even in patt. Rep last 2 rows once more. BO rem 4 (6-6-8-8) sts.

shape front neck (RHS) as follows:
Slip center 15 sts onto a stitch holder and rejoin yarn.

RS row: p6, k3, p1, ssk, knit to end.

WS row: p23 (28-32-35-39), k1, p3, k6.

RS row: BO 2 sts at beg row, p3 (4 sts on RH needle), k3, p1, ssk, knit to end.

WS row: p22 (27-31-34-38), k1, p3, k4.

RS row: BO 2 sts at beg row, p1 (2 sts on RH needle), k3, p1, ssk, knit to end, 27 (32-36-39-43) sts rem.

WS row: purl to last 6 sts, k1, p3, k2.

RS row: p2, k3, p1, ssk, knit to end.

Rep the last 2 rows 12 (13-15-16-16) more times, 14 (18-20-22-26) sts rem.

WS row: purl to last 6 sts, k1, p3, k2.

RS row: p2, k3, p1, knit to end.

Rep last 2 rows until armhole measures the same as back before shoulder shaping, end WS row facing for next row.

shape shoulder as follows:
BO 5 (6-7-7-9) sts at beg of next row. Work RS row even in patt. Rep last 2 rows once more. BO rem 4 (6-6-8-8) sts.

NECKBAND AND FINISHING

Weave in ends. Block pieces to given dimensions. Join LHS shoulder seam.

With RS facing, using 2.5 mm needles and beg at RH shoulder, pick up and knit 8 sts down RHS back neck, knit across 47 (49-53-55-55) sts from back neck stitch holder, pick up and knit 8 sts up LHS back neck, pick up and knit 30 (30-32-34-40) sts down LHS front neck, knit across 15 sts from front neck stitch holder, and pick up and knit 31 (31-33-35-41) st up RHS front neck, 139 (141-149-155-167) sts total.

WS row: *p2tog, yo, rep from * to last st, p1.

Knit 1 row. BO all sts knitwise.

Join RHS shoulder seam. With RS facing, using 2.5 mm needles, beg at bottom of armhole, pick up and knit 120 (120-126-130-140) sts around armhole edge. Knit 1 row. BO all sts knitwise. Rep for second armhole. Join side seams. Press lightly, following the instructions on the yarn label.

mindfulness pointer: let it flow

There are many times during a project when you may encounter an obstacle—the yarn store doesn't have the color you wanted, you want to complete a pattern repeat but are too tired, or you had hoped to finish the project to wear to your friend's wedding, but you have run out of time. If obstacles do present themselves, try to accept the options that are open to you. Pay attention to the reactions you have. Would it make you feel better to let go of a sense of control and simply go with the flow?

open to change

Habits can become like ruts, ingrained within us. The deeper a groove is cut, the harder it can be to deviate from it, to find another path to follow. We are all creatures of habit, but some of us find it especially challenging to even think about initiating a change. Even when we feel it is time, we go through a lot of vacillating before we commit to anything.

Until we ultimately make a decision, the possibilities are open. As we weigh the pros and cons, we communicate our indecision with our body language; yes and no are conveyed with definite movements, but our heads tilt from side to side and our hands waver to indicate a maybe.

I drew upon this back-and-forth motion when selecting the cables for this project. The cable for the sleeves tips back and forth and includes eyelets to indicate possibility. Space always offers the possibility of either being filled or left empty. I also chose the simple cable used for the body of this sweater for its movement in each direction—maybe this way, maybe that way. Then I imagined that after all the deliberation, a decision was necessary, so two paths open on either side of the V-neck, again including eyelets to indicate possibility.

SIZES / FINISHED CHEST MEASUREMENTS

XS 35.5 in [90 cm]
Small 38 in [96.5 cm]
Medium 40 in [101.5 cm]
Large 43 in [109 cm]
XL 46 in [117 cm]
2X 48 in [122 cm]

Instructions are given for smallest size. If changes are necessary for larger sizes, instructions are given in ( ). Where there is only one set of figures, this applies to all sizes.

MATERIALS

Young Touch Cotton by Estelle Designs, shade 064, 12 (13-14-16-17-18) 50 g balls (100% mercerized cotton).

Pair of 3.75 mm needles, stitch holder, CN.

Yarn amounts given are based on average requirements and are approximate.

TENSION / GAUGE

26 sts and 31 rows = 4 in [10 cm] over body pattern

25 sts and 29 rows = 4 in [10 cm] over sleeve pattern

Take the time to check your gauge; change needle sizes if necessary to obtain correct gauge and garment size.

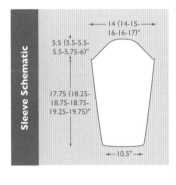

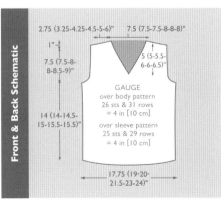

Symbols Used in These Charts

- ▪ p on RS; k on WS
- ☐ k on RS; p on WS
- ⊡ yfon
- ◩ ssk
- ◪ k2tog
- ⧄ C4B
- ⧄ C4F
- ⧄ C6B
- ⧄ C6F

Chart A

Chart reads R to L RS rows and L to R WS rows

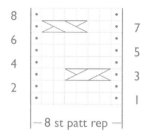

— 8 st patt rep —

Please see note on placing markers in
Things You Need to Know Before You Begin (p.8)

Chart B

Chart reads R to L RS rows and L to R WS rows

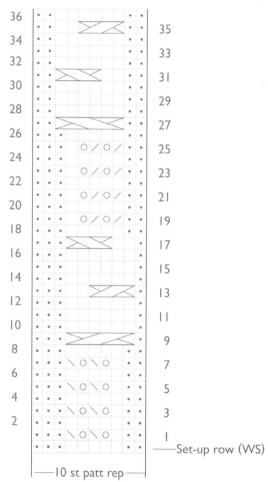

— 10 st patt rep —

Please see note on placing markers in
Things You Need to Know Before You Begin (p.8)

PATTERN A

Row 1 (RS): p1, k6, p1.

Row 2 and all WS rows: k1, p6, k1.

Row 3: p1, C4B, k2, p1.

Row 5: rep row 1.

Row 7: p1, k2, C4F, p1.

Rep rows 1–8 for patt A.

PATTERN B

Rows 1, 3, 5, and 7 (RS): p2, k1, (yfon, ssk) twice, p3.

Rows 2, 4, 6, and 8: k3, p5, k2.

Row 9: p1, C6B, p3.

Rows 10, 12, 14, and 16: k3, p6, k1.

Rows 11 and 15: p1, k6, p3.

Row 13: p1, C4B, k2, p3.

Row 17: p1, k2, C4F, p3.

Rows 18, 20, 22, 24, and 26: as row 2.

Rows 19, 21, 23, and 25: p2, (k2tog, yfon) twice, k1, p3.

Row 27: p2, C6F, p2.

Rows 28, 30, 32, 34, and 36: k2, p6, k2.

Rows 29 and 33: p2, k6, p2.

Row 31: p2, k2, C4F, p2.

Row 35: p2, C4B, k2, p2.

Rep rows 1–36 for patt B.

BACK

With 3.75 mm needles, cast on 116 (124-132-140-148-156) sts and knit 1 row.

work lower edge eyelet pattern as follows:

RS: p3 (7-3-7-3-7), *k1, yfon, ssk, k2tog, yfon, k1, p2, rep from * to last 1 (5-1-5-1-5) sts, p1 (5-1-5-1-5).

WS: k3 (7-3-7-3-7), *p6, k2, rep from * to last 1 (5-1-5-1-5) sts, k1 (5-1-5-1-5).

Rep the last 2 rows twice more.

now place cable pattern as follows:

Row 1 (RS): p2 (6-2-6-2-6), (work 8 st patt rep row 1 Chart A) 14 (14-16-16-18-18) times, p2 (6-2-6-2-6).

Row 2: k2 (6-2-6-2-6), (work 8 st patt rep row 2 Chart A) 14 (14-16-16-18-18) times, k2 (6-2-6-2-6).

Cont working Chart A rows in sequence as set until piece measures 14 (14-14.5-15-15.5-15.5) in [35.5 (35.5-37-38-39-39) cm], end with RS row facing for next row.

shape armholes as follows:

Cont in patt as set, BO 3 sts at beg of next 4 rows. Then dec 1 st at each end of following 10 (10-8-8-9-7) rows, 84 (92-104-112-118-130) sts rem.

Cont working in patt until armhole measures 7.5 (7.5-8-8.5-8.5-9) in [19 (19-20-21.5-21.5-23) cm] from beg of shaping, end with RS row facing for next row.

shape shoulders as follows:

Cont in patt as set, BO 6 (7-9-10-11-13) sts at beg of next 6 rows. BO rem 48 (50-50-52-52-52) sts.

FRONT

Work as back until armhole shaping is complete, then work even until completion of next row 4 of patt.

shape v neck (LHS):

RS row: work in patt across 30 (34-40-44-47-53) sts, p2tog, k2, yfon, ssk, k2tog, yfon, k2, p2tog, turn (this is neck edge).

Leave rem 42 (46-52-56-59-65) sts on a spare needle.

WS row: k1, p8, k2togb, work in patt to end.

RS row: work in patt to last 11 sts, p2tog, k2, yfon, ssk, k2tog, yfon, k2, p1.

Rep the last 2 rows 3 more times, 32 (36-42-46-49-55) sts rem.

WS row: k1, p8, k1, work to end in patt.

RS row: work as previous RS row.

Rep these 2 rows 13 (14-14-15-15-15) more times, 18 (21-27-30-33-39) sts rem. Work even in patt as now set until armhole measures the same as back before shoulder shaping, end with RS row facing for next row.

shape shoulder as follows:

Cont working in patt, BO 6 (7-9-10-11-13) sts at beg of row. Work WS row even. Rep these 2 rows once more. BO rem 6 (7-9-10-11-13) sts.

shape v neck (RHS):

Return to sts on spare needle, rejoin yarn at CF and work as follows:

RS row: p2togb, k2, yfon, ssk,

k2tog, yfon, k2, p2togb, work in patt to end.

WS row: work in patt to last 11 sts, k2togb, p8, k1.

RS row: p1, k2, yfon, ssk, k2tog, yfon, k2, p2togb, work in patt to end.

Rep the last 2 rows 3 more times, 32 (36-42-46-49-55) sts rem.

WS row: work in patt to last 10 sts, k1, p8, k1.

RS row: work as previous RS row.

Rep these 2 rows 13 (14-14-15-15-15) more times, 18 (21-27-30-33-39) sts rem. Work even in patt as now set until armhole measures the same as the back before shoulder shaping, end WS row facing for next row.

shape shoulder as follows:
Cont working in patt, BO 6 (7-9-10-11-13) sts at beg of row. Work RS row even. Rep these 2 rows once more. BO rem 6 (7-9-10-11-13) sts.

SLEEVE (MAKE 2 ALIKE)

Using 3.75 mm needles, cast on 66 sts, knit 1 row. Place patt as follows:

Set-up row (WS): k3, (k3, p5, k2) 6 times, k3.

Row 1 (RS): p3, work 10 st patt rep row 1 Chart B 6 times, p3.

Cont working Chart B rows in sequence as set, *at the same time* inc 1 st at each end of row 7 (9-5-5-5-5) and every following 10 (10-10-6-6-6)th row 4 (4-7-4-1-13) times, 76 (76-82-76-70-94) sts. Work all inc sts in rev St St throughout. Then inc 1 st at each end of every following 12th (12-8-8-8-8) row 6 (6-6-12-15-6) times, 88 (88-94-100-100-106) sts. Work even until sleeve measures 17.75 (18.25-18.75-18.75-19.25-19.75) in [45 (46-47.5-47.5-49-50) cm] from beg, end with RS row facing for next row.

shape cap as follows:
Cont working in patt, BO 3 sts at beg of next 4 rows. Dec 1 st at

each end of RS rows 13 (13-13-13-14-15) times. Dec 1 st at each end of next 6 rows. BO 5 (5-6-7-7-8) sts at beg of next 4 rows. BO rem 18 (18-20-22-20-20) sts.

FINISHING AND NECKBAND

Weave in ends. Block pieces to given dimensions.

Join RHS shoulder seam. Using 3.75 mm needles, beg at LH shoulder, pick up and knit 40 (39-42-47-47-50) sts down LH front and 40 (39-42-47-47-50) sts up RH front, pick up and knit 48 (50-50-52-52-52) sts across back neck, 128 (128-134-146-146-152) sts total.

work edging as follows:
BO 2 sts, * slip st back onto LH needle and cast on 2 sts, BO 5 sts, rep from * to end.

Join rem shoulder seam. Set sleeves into armholes. Join side and sleeve seams. Press lightly, following the instructions on the yarn label.

mindfulness pointer: expanding possibilities

Consider how the eyelets cause the knitted fabric to expand, the exact opposite effect of the contraction caused by the cables. Be mindful of how this mirrors our own lives. Have you ever noticed how even considering an alternate path can open us up, expand our world, and perhaps even increase our tolerance? Just being open to the possibility of change or new ways of looking at something can cause us to expand as people. While you work on this project, take a look at one of the more challenging projects in this book and consider it for your next creation.

practice makes perfect

The more we practice a skill or technique, the better we become, no matter how accomplished we are to begin with. During our practice, usually at the very moment when we believe we are beginning to get the hang of something, we goof. This isn't really a step backward; it's more like a retracing of our path. As I thought about this, I realized that we aren't retracing the exact same path, because we have learned something since the last time. It is more like climbing a spiral staircase. After we complete one rotation, the view is almost the same—but not quite.

In its simplest form, a cable mimics two cords twisting around each other, and if you follow the path of one of these cords, it appears to form a spiral. As these ideas gelled in my mind, I decided to include a basic project that would act as a teaching tool and allow for plenty of time to practice. A scarf was the obvious choice, as its length gives plenty of room to repeat a pattern over and over.

To make the scarf, you begin with the simplest of cables and proceed through several other variations. When you have completed the first half, you will have attempted all the principal techniques used in cable knitting. You can continue to practice by completing the second half and then making the hat. Along the way, you will find notes that I have included to explain how the different variations relate to each other. If you study what is happening, the mystery of cable knitting will be revealed to you.

SIZES

Both pieces one size: Scarf measures 10 in [25 cm] wide by 60 in [152 cm] long

Hat measures 19 in [48 cm] in circumference, 7 in [18 cm] high

MATERIALS

Wings by Classic Elite Yarns, shade 2353, 3 skeins for scarf, 2 skeins for hat (55% alpaca, 23% silk, 22% wool).

Pair of 4.5 mm needles, CN, blunt sewing needle for grafting scarf.

Yarn amounts given are based on average requirements and are approximate.

TENSION / GAUGE

24 sts and 28 rows = 4 in [10 cm] over cable pattern.

Take the time to check your gauge; change needle sizes if necessary to obtain correct gauge and garment size.

REFER TO GLOSSARY ON PAGE 13 FOR: SEED STITCH.

Symbols Used in This Chart

⊡	p on RS; k on WS
▱	T3B
▱	C4B
▱	T4B
▢	k on RS; p on WS
▱	T3F
▱	C4F
▱	T4F

Chart reads R to L RS rows and L to R WS rows

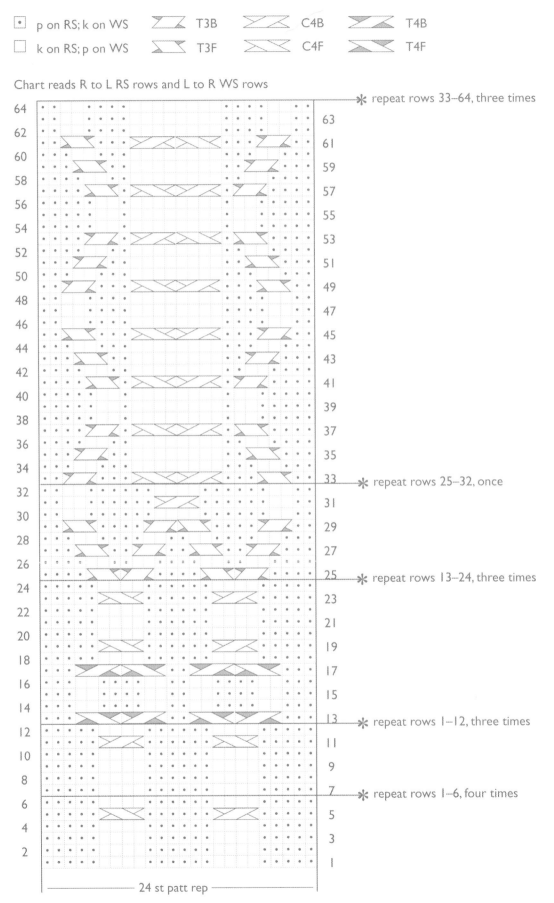

✳ repeat rows 33–64, three times

✳ repeat rows 25–32, once

✳ repeat rows 13–24, three times

✳ repeat rows 1–12, three times

✳ repeat rows 1–6, four times

— 24 st patt rep —

Please see note on placing markers in Things You Need to Know Before You Begin (p. 8)

CABLE PATTERN

Row 1 (RS): p5, k4, p6, k4, p5.

Row 2: k5, p4, k6, p4, k5.

Rows 3 and 4: rep rows 1 and 2.

Row 5: p5, C4B, p6, C4F, p5.

Row 6: rep row 2.

Rows 7–10: rep rows 1–4.

Row 11: p5, C4F, p6, C4B, p5.

Row 12: rep row 2.

Row 13: p3, T4B, T4F, p2, T4B, T4F, p3.

Row 14: k3, p2, k4, p2, k2, p2, k4, p2, k3.

Row 15: p3, k2, p4, k2, p2, k2, p4, k2, p3.

Row 16: rep row 14.

Row 17: p3, T4F, T4B, p2, T4F, T4B, p3.

Row 18: rep row 2.

Row 19: rep row 5.

Row 20: rep row 2.

Rows 21 and 22: rep rows 1 and 2.

Row 23: rep row 5.

Row 24: rep row 2.

Row 25: (p4, T3B, T3F) twice, p4.

Row 26: (k4, p2, k2, p2) twice, k4.

Row 27: p3, T3B, p2, T3F, p2, T3B, p2, T3F, p3.

Row 28: k3, p2, k4, p2, k2, p2, k4, p2, k3.

Row 29: p2, (T3B, p4, T3F) twice, p2.

Row 30: k2, p2, k6, p4, k6, p2, k2.

Row 31: p2, k2, p6, C4B, p6, k2, p2.

Row 32: rep row 30.

Row 33: p2, T3F, p3, C4B, C4F, p3, T3B, p2.

Row 34: k3, p2, k3, p8, k3, p2, k3.

Row 35: p3, T3F, p2, k8, p2, T3B, p3.

Row 36: k4, p2, k2, p8, k2, p2, k4.

Row 37: p4, T3F, p1, C4B, C4F, p1, T3B, p4.

Row 38: k5, p2, k1, p8, k1, p2, k5.

Row 39: p5, k2, p1, k8, p1, k2, p5.

Row 40: rep row 38.

Row 41: p4, T3B, p1, C4B, C4F, p1, T3F, p4.

Row 42: rep row 36.

Row 43: p3, T3B, p2, k8, p2, T3F, p3.

Row 44: rep row 34.

Row 45: p2, T3B, p3, C4B, C4F, p3, T3F, p2.

Row 46: k2, p2, k4, p8, k4, p2, k2.

Row 47: p2, k2, p4, k8, p4, k2, p2.

Row 48: rep row 46.

Rows 49–52: rep rows 33–36.

Row 53: p4, T3F, p1, C4F, C4B, p1, T3B, p4.

Rows 54–60: rep rows 38–44.

Row 61: p2, T3B, p3, C4F, C4B, p3, T3F, p2.

Rows 62–64: rep rows 46–48. Rep rows as given in instructions.

SCARF (MAKE 2 PIECES ALIKE)

Using 4.5 mm needles, cast on 60 sts, work 4 rows in seed stitch.

place cable panels as follows:

RS row: (k1, p1) 3 times, (work 24 st patt rep row 1 of chart) twice, (k1, p1) 3 times.

WS row: (p1, k1) 3 times, (work 24 st patt rep row 2 of chart) twice, (p1, k1) 3 times.

Then work as follows: cont with cable panels as set, work until row 6 of chart is complete, followed by rows 1–6, 3 more times—24 rows worked total.

Then work rows 1–12 3 times—60 rows worked total.

Work rows 13–24 3 times—96 rows worked total.

Work rows 25–32 once—104 rows worked total.

Work rows 33–64, 3 times—200 rows worked total.

Leave sts on a stitch holder.

Once you have made both pieces, graft them tog at CB. Slip each set of sts from each stitch holder onto a separate needle. With both needles pointing in the same direction, place the 2 pieces top edge to top edge with RS facing up; *do not arrange pieces* back to back as for sewing a seam.

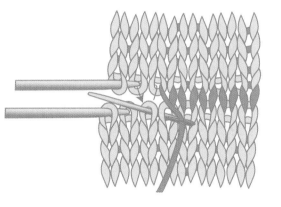

Use a blunt sewing needle threaded with a length of yarn approx 50 in [127 cm].

Bring needle up through first stitch on first side of scarf. Then insert the needle down through the first loop on second side of scarf and bring up needle through second loop on second side. Then insert needle back down into first loop on first side and bring up needle through second loop on first side. Then insert needle down into second loop on second side and up through the third loop on the second side. Continue in this way

until all stitches have been grafted together. Allow each st to slip off the needle once it has been secured. Adjust the tension of your stitching at intervals to ensure a smooth, unwrinkled join. Block scarf to given dimensions.

HAT

Using 4.5 mm needles cast on 110 sts, work 4 rows in seed stitch, inc 10 sts evenly across 4th row—120 sts.

RS row: (work 24 st patt rep row 1 of chart) 5 times.

WS row: (work 24 st patt rep row 2 of chart) 5 times.

Cont working chart rows in sequence as set until row 48 has been completed. BO all sts.

finishing

Block piece to given dimensions. Join 2 short edges tog to form a tube. Place flat with seam at CB. Join top seam (BO edge). Make 2 tassels and sew to points.

As you knit, take special note of what you are practicing in each section:

Rows 1–6: here is the most basic twist, in opposing directions. Notice how taking the sts to the back or front when you cross them changes the direction of the twist. When you repeat the same cross one above the other, a clas-

sic rope pattern is formed.

Rows 1–12: when you combine opposite twists vertically, it produces a wave rather than a rope.

Rows 13–24: when you work knit and purl stitches within the cross, it appears to make the cords move across the fabric; in this case they move away from each other then back together again.

Rows 25–32: by using a modification of the cross used in rows 13-24, the cords move out across the fabric but at a different speed from before, changing the angle created.

Rows 33–48: use the same cables used in rows 1–6, but as there is no reverse stockinette stitch between them, they butt up to each other and create a new pattern.

Rows 49–64: placed as in rows 33–48, but when you change the direction of the crosses working vertically, an entirely different pattern is formed.

As you reach each change in the pattern, you may choose to continue repeating the previous pattern until you feel you have mastered it. If you do add more repeats to your scarf, it will turn out longer and use more yarn. But you may modify the ending point to achieve your desired length.

mindfulness pointer: spiral learning

One of my students once commented that my perpetual optimism had made a strong impression on him (yes, *him*). He made this comment when I was pointing out that even though he had just made a mistake, his error was now presenting a great opportunity for learning. An experienced knitter is, therefore, somebody who has made many mistakes, and—more important—continues to do so, constantly challenging himself with his chosen projects. If you make a mistake while working on this project, use it as an opportunity to watch what your reactions are. Are you easily able to reframe the error as an opportunity to learn? If you do work up the project without errors, then congratulate yourself on having practiced sufficiently and on having made enough mistakes previously to have achieved this level of skill.

gathering intentions

We think of a change occurring after participating in an activity for a period of time. But before we can precipitate a change, it is necessary to first spend some time thinking, planning, or simply gathering momentum. We describe this as establishing an intention, which of course can be bad or good, but for our purposes, we will assume the latter. I am thinking in particular of those moments when we decide, "This is it!" I am going to save for something, I am going to attend a class regularly, I will lose that ten pounds, I will stop biting my nails, or I will write that book I have always dreamed of. In that one instant you cause a shift in your thinking, which brings about action.

I sometimes use I-cords when experimenting with cable twists and interlacing patterns. I have come to see I-cords as cables that just haven't formed themselves into patterns yet. They are a little like the scattered thoughts that we have before we draw them together and set our intention to make a change in our lives.

So in this garment I have used I-cords attached to the lower sections that appear to then form themselves into cables. This represents the thought process that occurs before a change is precipitated and goes on to become set into a regular pattern.

SIZES / FINISHED CHEST MEASUREMENTS

Small 36 in [91.5 cm]
Medium 40 in [101.5 cm]
Large 44 in [112 cm]
XL 48 in [122 cm]
2X 52 in [132 cm]

Instructions are given for smallest size. If changes are necessary for larger sizes, the instructions are given in ( ). Where there is only one set of figures, this applies to all sizes.

MATERIALS

18/24 Wool by Mission Falls, shade 020 Cornflower, 14 (15-17-18-20) 50 g balls (100% superwash merino wool).

Pair of 5 mm needles, CN, 2 stitch holders.

Yarn amounts given are based on average requirements and are approximate.

TENSION / GAUGE

23 sts and 28 rows = 4 in [10 cm] over cable pattern.

Take the time to check your gauge; change needle sizes if necessary to obtain correct gauge and garment size.

REFER TO GLOSSARY ON PAGE 13 FOR: SEED STITCH, AND TO TECHNIQUES ON PAGE 12 FOR I-CORD.

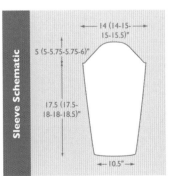

Sleeve Schematic

14 (14-15-15-15.5)"

5 (5-5.75-5.75-6)"

17.5 (17.5-18-18-18.5)"

10.5"

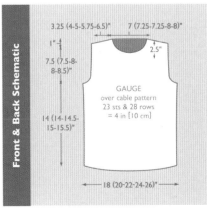

Front & Back Schematic

3.25 (4-5-5.75-6.5)"   7 (7.25-7.25-8-8)"

1"

2.5"

7.5 (7.5-8-8-8.5)"

GAUGE
over cable pattern
23 sts & 28 rows
= 4 in [10 cm]

14 (14-14.5-15-15.5)"

18 (20-22-24-26)"

Symbols Used in These Charts

- ⊡ p on RS; k on WS
- ☐ k on RS; p on WS
- ⬓ T3B
- ⬓ T3F
- ⬓ C4B

Chart A

Chart reads R to L RS rows and L to R WS rows

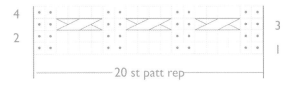

20 st patt rep

Chart B

Chart reads R to L RS rows and L to R WS rows

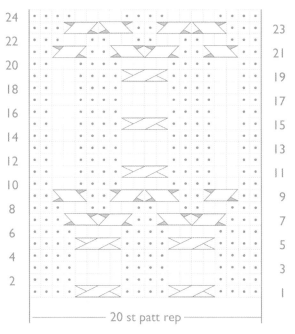

20 st patt rep

Please see note on placing markers in
Things You Need to Know Before You Begin (p.8)

PATTERN A

Row 1 (RS): (p2, k4) 3 times, p2.

Row 2: (k2, p4) 3 times, k2.

Row 3: (p2, C4B) 3 times, p2.

Row 4: rep row 2.

Rep rows 1–4 for patt A.

PATTERN B

Row 1 (RS): (p4, C4B) twice, p4.

Row 2: (k4, p4) twice, k4.

Row 3: (p4, k4) twice, p4.

Rows 4–6: rep row 2, then rows 1 and 2 once more.

Row 7: p3, (T3B, T3F, p2) twice, p1.

Row 8: k3, (p2, k2) 3 times, p2, k3.

Row 9: p2, (T3B, p2, T3F) twice, p2.

Row 10: k2, p2, k4, p4, k4, p2, k2.

Row 11: p2, k2, p4, C4B, p4, k2, p2.

Row 12: rep row 10.

Row 13: p2, k2, p4, k4, p4, k2, p2.

Row 14: rep row 10.

Rows 15–20: rep rows 11–14, then rows 11 and 12 once more.

Row 21: p2, (T3F, p2, T3B) twice, p2.

Row 22: rep row 8.

Row 23: p3, (T3F, T3B, p2) twice, p1.

Row 24: rep row 2.

Rep rows 1–24 for patt B.

BACK

Using 5 mm needles, cast on 104 (116-126-138-148) sts.

Work 1 row in seed st, then set up pattern as follows:

RS row: p4 (10-15-21-26), *(k4, p2) twice, k4, p6, k4, p4, k4, p6, rep from * once more, (k4, p2) twice, k4, p4 (10-15-21-26).

WS row: k4 (10-15-21-26), *(p4, k2) twice, p4, k6, p4, k4, p4, k6, rep from * once more, (p4, k2) twice, p4, k4 (10-15-21-26).

place cable panels as follows:
Row 1 (RS): p2 (8-13-19-24), (work 20 st patt rep row 1 Chart A, then 20 st patt rep row 1 Chart B) twice, then work 20 sts patt rep row 1 Chart A once more, p2 (8-13-19-24).

Row 2: k2 (8-13-19-24), (work 20 st patt rep row 2 Chart A, then 20 st patt rep row 2 Chart B) twice, then work 20 st patt rep row 2 Chart A once more, k2 (8-13-19-24).

Cont working chart rows in sequence in patt as set, until work measures 14 (14-14.5-15-15.5) in [35.5 (35.5-37-38-39) cm], end RS row facing for next row.

shape armholes as follows:
Cont in patt, BO 5 sts at beg of next 2 rows, 4 sts at beg of following 2 rows, then 3 sts at beg of next 2 rows. Dec 1 st at each end of next row, 78 (90-100-112-122) sts rem.

Cont working even in patt until armhole measures 7.5 (7.5-8-8-8.5) in [19 (19-20-20-21.5) cm] from beg of shaping.

shape shoulders as follows:
BO 6 (8-10-11-13) sts at beg of next 4 rows, then BO 7 (8-9-11-12) sts at beg of following 2 rows. Leave rem 40 (42-42-46-46) sts on a stitch holder.

FRONT

Using 5 mm needles, cast on 104 (116-126-138-148) sts.

Work 1 row in seed st, then set up pattern as follows:

Row 1 (RS): p2 (8-13-19-24), work 20 st patt rep row 1 Chart A, place marker, p20, place second marker, work 20 st patt rep row 1 Chart A, then work 20 st patt rep row 1 Chart B, followed by 20 st patt rep row 1 Chart A once more, p2 (8-13-19-24).

Row 2: k2 (8-13-19-24), work 20 st patt rep row 2 Chart A, then 20 st patt rep row 2 Chart B, followed by 20 st patt rep Chart A once more, k20, then work 20 st patt rep row 2 Chart A, k2 (8-13-19-24).

Cont working chart rows in sequence as set, following instructions given for each chart in sequence over first 19 rows and working sts between markers purl on RS rows, knit on WS rows.

Cont working Chart A in sequence, place second Chart B panel as follows:

Row 20 (WS): k2 (8-13-19-24), (work 20 st patt rep Chart A, then as given row 20 Chart B) twice, then 20 st patt Chart A once more, k2 (8-13-19-24).

Row 21: p2 (8-13-19-24), (work 20 st patt rep Chart A, then as given row 21 Chart B) twice, then work 20 st patt rep Chart A once more, p2 (8-13-19-24).

Cont working chart rows in sequence as <u>now</u> set, until work measures 14 (14-14.5-15-15.5) in [35.5 (35.5-37-38-39.25) cm], end with RS row facing for next row.

work armhole shaping
as given for back. Then cont in patt as set until armhole measures approx 5 (5-5.5-5.5-6) in [13 (13-14-14-15) cm] from beg of shaping, end row 1 Chart A facing for next row.

shape front neck as follows:
Cont in patt work across 30 (36-41-47-52) sts, turn (this is neck edge), leave rem 48 (54-59-65-70) sts on a spare needle.

Working on the 30 (36-41-47-52) sts only, dec 1 st at neck edge on next 11 (12-12-14-14) rows, 19 (24-29-33-38) sts rem. Work even until armhole measures the same as back before shoulder shaping, end RS row facing for next row.

shape shoulder as follows:
BO 6 (8-10-11-13) sts at beg of next row. Work WS row even. Rep the last 2 rows once more. BO rem 7 (8-9-11-12) sts.

Return to sts on spare needle, slip center 18 sts onto a stitch holder, rejoin yarn, work to end. Dec 1 st at neck edge on next 11 (12-12-14-14) rows, 19 (24-29-33-38) sts rem. Work even until armhole measures the same as back before shoulder shaping, end WS row facing for next row.

shape shoulder as follows:

BO 6 (8-10-11-13) sts at beg of next row. Work RS even. Rep the last 2 rows once more. BO rem 7 (8-9-11-12) sts.

SLEEVE (RHS)

Using 5 mm needles, cast on 60 sts.

Work 1 row in seed st, then set up pattern as follows:

Row 1 (RS): work 20 st patt rep row 1 Chart A, then 20 st patt rep row 1 Chart B, then work 20 st patt rep row 1 Chart A once more.

Row 2: work 20 st patt rep row 2 Chart A, then 20 st patt rep row 2 Chart B, then work 20 st patt rep row 2 Chart A once more.

Cont working chart rows in sequence as set, *at the same time* inc 1 st at each end of row 5 and every following 12th (12-8-8-8) row 9 (9-5-5-14) times, 80 (80-72-72-90) sts, work all inc sts in rev St St throughout. Then inc 1 st at each end of every following 0th (0-10-10-0) row 0 (0-7-7-0) times, 80 (80-86-86-90) sts. Work even until sleeve measures

17.5 (17.5-18-18-18.5) in [44.5 (44.5-45.5-45.5-47) cm] from beg, end with RS row facing for next row.

shape cap as follows:

Cont in patt as set, BO 4 sts at beg of next 2 rows, 3 (3-4-4-5) sts at beg of following 2 rows, 2 sts at beg of following 4 rows. Dec 1 st at each end of following 12 (12-14-14-15) RS rows, 34 sts rem. BO 4 sts at beg of next 4 rows. BO rem 18 sts.

SLEEVE (LHS)

Using 5 mm needles, cast on 60 sts.

Work 1 row in seed st, then set up pattern as follows:

Row 1 (RS): work 20 st patt rep row 1 Chart A, place marker, p20, place second marker, then work 20 st patt rep row 1 Chart A once more.

Row 2: work 20 st patt rep row 2 Chart A, k20, then work 20 st patt rep row 2 Chart A once more.

Cont working chart rows in sequence as set, following instructions given for chart in sequence over first 19 rows and working sts between markers purl on RS rows, knit on WS rows, *at the same time* inc 1 st at each end of row 5 and row 17 (17-13-13-13), work all inc sts in rev St St throughout.

Cont working Chart A in sequence, place Chart B panel as follows:

Row 20: p2, work 20 st patt rep Chart A, then 20 st patt rep row 20 Chart B, then work 20 st patt rep Chart A once more, p2.

Row 21: sizes L, XL, and 2X only work inc in 1st st, **all sizes,** k2 (2-1-1-1), work 20 st patt rep Chart A, then 20 st patt rep row 21 Chart B, then work 20 st patt rep Chart A once more, k2 (2-1-1-1), **sizes XL and 2X only** inc 1 st in last st.

Cont working chart rows in sequence as <u>now</u> set, *at the same time* inc 1 st at each end of row 29 and every following 12th (12-8-8-8) row 7 (7-2-2-11) times, 80 (80-72-72-90) sts. Then inc 1 st at each end of every following 0th (0-10-10-0) row 0 (0-7-7-0) times, 80 (80-86-86-90) sts. Work even without further inc until sleeve measures 17.5 (17.5-18-18-18.5) in [44.5 (44.5-45.5-45.5-47) cm] from beg.

shape cap as given for RH sleeve

FINISHING AND NECKLINE

Weave in ends. Block out pieces to given dimensions.

Join RH shoulder seam.

Using 5 mm needles, with RS facing, beg at LH shoulder, pick up and knit 21 (20-20-24-24) sts down LHS front neck, work across 18 sts from front neck stitch holder in patt, pick up and knit 21 (20-20-24-24) sts up RHS front neck, work across 40

(42-42-46-46) sts from back neck stitch holder in patt, 100 (100-100-112-112) sts total.

Work back and forth as follows:

WS row: k0 (1-1-3-3), p2, k4, p2, k2, work in patt as Chart A across next 20 sts, k2, (p2, k4) 4 (4-4-5-5) times, p2, k2, work in patt as Chart A across next 20 sts, k2, (p2, k4) 2 (2-2-3-3) times, p2, k4 (3-3-1-1).

RS row: p4 (3-3-1-1), k2, (p4, k2) 2 (2-2-3-3) times, p2, work in patt as Chart A across next 20 sts, p2, k2, (p4, k2) 4 (4-4-5-5) times, p2, work in patt as Chart A across next 20 sts, p2, k2, p4, k2, p0 (1-1-3-3).

Rep these 2 rows 7 more times. BO in patt.

Join rem shoulder and turtleneck seam. Set sleeves into armholes. Join side and sleeve seams.

Make four 3 st I-cords each approx 12 in [30.5 cm] long.

Working at lower edge of front. Attach I-cords and gather lower edge as shown in diagram.

Repeat with the other two I-cords at lower edge on LH sleeve.

Press lightly, following the instructions on the yarn label.

Stage 1

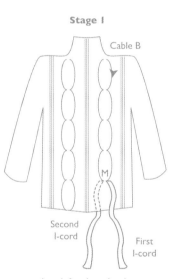

Cable B

Second I-cord

First I-cord

Attach first I-cord to bottom center of cable B, point marked M to RS of fabric. Attach a second I-cord at same point to WS of fabric.

Stage 2

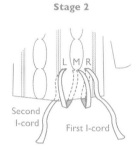

Second I-cord

First I-cord

Take first I-cord around lower cast-on edge to WS. Thread through knitting at point R and bring back to RS.

Take second I-cord around lower cast-on edge to RS. Thread through knitting at point L and bring back to WS.

Stage 3

First I-cord

Second I-cord

Pull slightly on the cords to draw up the lower edge. Take ends of I-cords and thread them through both the loops formed at lower edge. (They will be threading in opposite directions.)

Stage 4

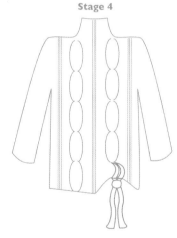

Then tie them into a loose knot. Adjust the cords to look pleasing.

mindfulness pointer: knitting with intent

Try deciding what your intentions for this project are as you begin. Have an intention for how great you will look wearing it, how happy the recipient of the gift will be, how great you will feel having learned to knit cables well. As you work the first few rows, the intention will become set into the fabric as you learn the pattern. As you progress, how does it feel to keep returning to the pattern? Some days you may be less enthused. Is avoiding the project like eating a huge piece of chocolate cake on the road to losing that ten pounds? Remember your intentions, and get back to the pattern tomorrow. Before you know it, your intentions will be fulfilled.

inspired by nature

WE RESPOND TO THE ORGANIC, TEXTURAL PATTERNS FORMED BY
NATURE—MOST NOTABLY IN TREES AND THEIR BARK—IN AN
INSTINCTIVE WAY, FINDING PLEASURE AND COMFORT IN THEM.
THESE TEXTURES AND PATTERNS CAN BE MIRRORED BY THE
INHERENT TACTILE QUALITIES OF CABLE-KNIT FABRICS.

Whether of color, form, texture, line, or shape, the natural world
presents the artist with infinite variety. I have let nature's paint box and
pattern book inspire my design choices—I've used unusual color palettes
from rocks and flowers, and I've let organic structures influence the sil-
houette of a garment.

Knitters are very tactile: we focus on the sensation of yarn running
through our fingers and can determine fiber composition by feel.
Knowing this, I had a strong feeling that creating patterns inspired by
the beauty and variety of textures found in tree bark would be very
appealing to most knitters. I was overtaken by the urge to figure out how
to incorporate or translate that beauty into knitted fabric.

To maintain the feeling of an organic pattern while keeping the
instructions user-friendly, I decided it was necessary to bring some repetition to any interpretation of these textures. To achieve this, I nar-
rowed my focus, zooming in on smaller elements and forming repeats
with them. My selection of yarn and trim details was also inspired by the
texture and beauty of trees.

wrap yourself in nature

We embrace the advent of new technology and the possibilities it presents. But even though we've seen some fabulous innovations in textiles, such as microfibers and polar fleece, we still return to using traditional fibers like wool and cotton. Is this because they impart harmony with nature?

We are comfortable being cocooned in natural surroundings. If you have ever slept in a log cabin, you know that its sounds, smells, and natural imperfections are different from the feel of a brick or concrete building's interior. These natural features bring us reassurance and reconnect us to what we instinctively know and understand.

I love simple garments that we pull around ourselves, reminding us of snuggling under blankets. This wrap, knitted in natural fibers, takes its inspiration from the organic tree patterns that I love so much. It is like being wrapped in nature. To further reinforce this nurturing, protective feeling, even the color—soft and muted—appears to have a natural patina. This wrap will keep out the chill and take the edge off the harshness of an industrial world.

MATERIALS

Sensation by Naturally, shade 303,12 x 50 g skeins (70% merino wool, 30% angora).

Pair of 5 mm needles, CN.

Yarn amounts given are based on average requirements and are approximate.

TENSION / GAUGE

24 sts and 26 rows = 4 in [10 cm] over cable pattern.

Take the time to check your gauge; change needle sizes if necessary to obtain correct gauge and garment size.

REFER TO GLOSSARY ON PAGE 13 FOR: SEED STITCH

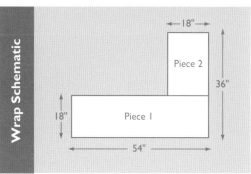

Wrap Schematic

Piece 2 — 18" — 36"

Piece 1 — 18" — 54"

PATTERN A

Row 1 (RS): (k1, p1) twice, T4F, p8.

Row 2: k8, p3, (k1, p1) twice, k1.

Row 3: (k1, p1) twice, T2B, T4F, p6.

Row 4: k6, p3, k2, p2, k1, p1, k1.

Row 5: (k1, p1) twice, T2F, T2B, T4F, p4.

Row 6: k4, p3, k2, C2BW, (k1, p1) twice, k1.

Row 7: (k1, p1) twice, T2B, T2F, T2B, T4F, p2.

Row 8: k2, p3, k2, C2FW, k2, p2, k1, p1, k1.

Row 9: (k1, p1) twice, (T2F, T2B) twice, T4F.

Row 10: p2, k3, C2BW, k2, C2BW, (k1, p1) twice, k1.

Row 11: (k1, p1) twice, (T2B, T2F) twice, T4B.

Row 12: k2, p3, k2, C2FW, k2, p2, k1, p1, k1.

Row 13: (k1, p1) twice, T2F, T2B, T2F, T4B, p2.

Row 14: k4, p3, k2, C2BW, (k1, p1) twice, k1.

Row 15: (k1, p1) twice, T2B, T2F, T4B, p4.

Row 16: k6, p3, k2, p2, k1, p1, k1.

Row 17: (k1, p1) twice, T2F, T4B, p6.

Row 18: k8, p3, (k1, p1) twice, k1.

Row 19: (k1, p1) twice, T4B, p8.

Row 20: k10, p3, k1, p1, k1.
Rep rows 1–20 for patt A.

PATTERN B

Row 1 (RS): p6, T5L, p2, C6F, p8.

Row 2: k8, p6, k2, p3, k8.

Row 3: p8, T5L, k6, p8.

Row 4: k8, p9, k10.

Row 5: p10, C6B, k3, p8.

Row 6: rep row 4.

Row 7: p10, k3, C6F, p8.

Row 8: rep row 4.

Row 9: p10, k6, T5L, p6.

Row 10: k6, p3, k2, p6, k10.

Row 11: p10, C6B, p2, T5L, p4.

Row 12: k4, p3, k4, p6, k10.

Row 13: p8, T5R, T5L, p2, k3, p4.

Row 14: k4, p3, k2, p3, k4, p3, k8.

Row 15: p6, T5R, p4, k3, p2, k3, p4.

Row 16: k4, p3, k2, (p3, k6) twice.

Row 17: p6, k3, p4, T5R, p2, k3, p4.

Row 18: (k4, p3) 3 times, k6.

Row 19: p6, T5L, T5R, p2, T5R, p4.

Row 20: k6, p3, k4, p6, k8.

Row 21: p8, C6B, p2, T5R, p6.

Row 22: k8, p3, k2, p6, k8.

Row 23: p8, k6, T5R, p8.

Row 24: k10, p9, k8.

Row 25: p8, k3, C6F, p10.

Row 26: rep row 24.

Row 27: p8, C6B, k3, p10.

Row 28: rep row 24.

Row 29: p6, T5R, k6, p10.

Row 30: k10, p6, k2, p3, k6.

Row 31: p4, T5R, p2, C6F, p10.

Row 32: k10, p6, k4, p3, k4.

Row 33: p4, k3, p2, T5R, T5L, p8.

Row 34: k8, p3, k4, p3, k2,

Symbols Used in These Charts

⊡ p on RS; k on WS	◪ T2B	◪ T4B	◪ T5R	◪ C6B
☐ k on RS; p on WS	◪ T2F	◪ T4F	◪ T5L	◪ C6F
	◪ C2BW			
	◪ C2FW			

Chart A

Chart reads R to L RS rows and L to R WS rows

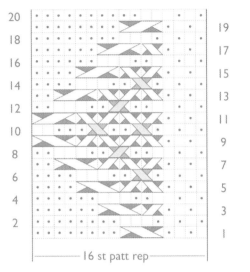

|— 16 st patt rep —|

Chart C

Chart reads R to L RS rows and L to R WS rows

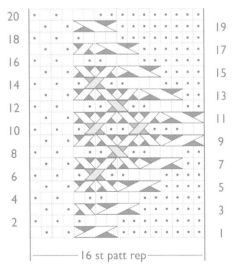

|— 16 st patt rep —|

Chart B

Chart reads R to L RS rows and L to R WS rows

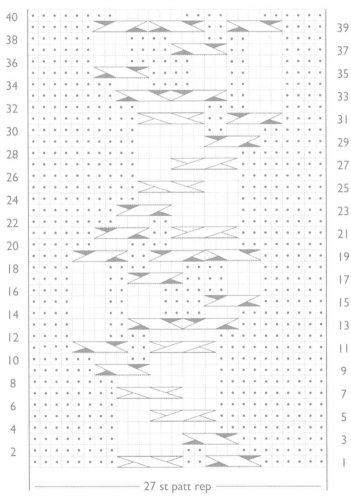

|— 27 st patt rep —|

Please see note on placing markers in
Things You Need to Know Before You Begin (p.8)

p3, k4.

Row 35: p4, k3, p2, k3, p4, T5L, p6.

Row 36: (k6, p3) twice, k2, p3, k4.

Row 37: p4, k3, p2, T5L, p4, k3, p6.

Row 38: k6, (p3, k4) 3 times.

Row 39: p4, T5L, p2, T5L, T5R, p6.

Row 40: k8, p6, k4, p3, k6.

Rep rows 1–40 for patt B.

PATTERN C

Row 1 (RS): p8, T4B, (p1, k1) twice.

Row 2: (k1, p1) twice, k1, p3, k8.

Row 3: p6, T4B, T2F, (p1, k1) twice.

Row 4: k1, p1, k1, p2, k2, p3, k6.

Row 5: p4, T4B, T2F, T2B, (p1, k1) twice.

Row 6: (k1, p1) twice, k1, C2FW, k2, p3, k4.

Row 7: p2, T4B, T2F, T2B, T2F, (p1, k1) twice.

Row 8: k1, p1, k1, p2, k2, C2BW, k2, p3, k2.

Row 9: T4B, (T2F, T2B) twice, (p1, k1) twice.

Row 10: (k1, p1) twice, k1, C2FW, k2, C2FW, k3, p2.

Row 11: T4F, (T2B, T2F) twice, (p1, k1) twice.

Row 12: k1, p1, k1, p2, k2, C2BW, k2, p3, k2.

Row 13: p2, T4F, T2B, T2F, T2B, (p1, k1) twice.

Row 14: (k1, p1) twice, k1, C2FW, k2, p3, k4.

Row 15: p4, T4F, T2B, T2F, (p1, k1) twice.

Row 16: k1, p1, k1, p2, k2, p3, k6.

Row 17: p6, T4F, T2B, (p1, k1) twice.

Row 18: (k1, p1) twice, k1, p3, k8.

Row 19: p8, T4F, (p1, k1) twice.

Row 20: k1, p1, k1, p3, k10.

Rep rows 1–20 for patt C.

PIECE ONE

Using 5 mm needles, cast on 113 sts, work 4 rows in seed st.

Work set-up rows as follows:

RS: (k1, p1) twice, k2, p16, (k3, p4, k6, p14) twice, k3, p4, k6, p18, k2, (p1, k1) twice.

WS: (k1, p1) twice, p2, k18, p6, k4, p3, (k14, p6, k4, p3) twice, k16, p2, (p1, k1) twice.

Then place pattern as follows:

RS: work 16 st patt rep row 1 Chart A, (work 27 st patt rep row 1 Chart B) 3 times, work 16 st patt

rep row 1 Chart C.

WS: work 16 st patt rep row 2 Chart C, (work 27 st patt rep row 2 Chart B) 3 times, work 16 st patt rep row 2 Chart A.

Cont working rows 3–20 in sequence given for each chart as set.

Then work rows 1–20 Charts A and C once more, at same time working rows 21–40 Chart B. Cont working in this way (Charts A and C worked twice for each rep of Chart B) until piece measures approx 54 in [137 cm] from beg, end having worked row 20 all charts. Work 4 rows in seed st. BO all sts.

PIECE TWO

Work as given for piece one until work measures approx 36 in [91 cm] from beg, end having worked row 20 all charts. BO all sts.

FINISHING

Weave in ends. Block each piece to dimensions given.

Sew piece two to piece one at right angles as indicated in diagram. Press lightly, following the instructions on the yarn label.

mindfulness pointer: cozy up and knit

We sometimes use the time we take to knit as a refuge from the outside world. Just like taking a bubble bath, this time can be a special treat, a getaway from chores or work, a time we take to nurture ourselves. So may I suggest that you knit this pattern during the long, cold winter months? Then you can enjoy the secondary benefit of being cocooned by the fabric sitting on your lap while you work. When I knitted this wrap, I certainly took pleasure in the physical comfort it brought. Take some time to shut out the harsh industrial world around you and immerse yourself in the project.

putting down roots

There is a sense of both expectation and anticipation when we plant a seed. This is followed by a period where little appears to be happening, where we have to simply trust in the process. I think you will agree that this is akin to casting on that initial row at the beginning of a knitting project.

We know that the first few rows will go slowly while we learn the pattern and get into a rhythm, like a seed germinating. Just as an ugly bulb or dry, uninspiring seed eventually delights us when it blooms, these rows will come to fruition as the pattern reveals itself. Often the cast-on edge can hardly be detected, but the roots of the pattern are certainly there.

This garment begins with a simple 2 x 2 rib fabric. The cast-on edge remains insignificant when worked in the same color, as on the body pieces. Your attention is drawn to it once you introduce a contrasting color. It becomes a feature. I used this effect for the cast-on edge of the sleeves. The I-cord trim added to this foundation reflects the root of the piece, and also references the gnarled roots of an old tree. It is repeated at the neckline, technically an ending, not a beginning, but you can grant me a little artistic license, can't you? Anyway, as this is the end of one project, it must also mean the beginning of a new one!

SIZES / FINISHED CHEST
MEASUREMENTS

XS 30 in [76 cm]

Small 34 in [86 cm]

Medium 38 in [96.5 cm]

Large 43 in [109 cm]

XL 46 in [117 cm]

2X 49 in [125 cm]

Instructions are given for smallest size. If changes are necessary for larger sizes, the instructions are given in ( ). Where there is only one set of figures, this applies to all sizes.

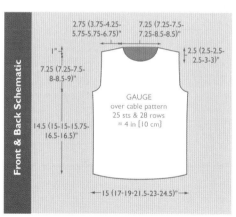

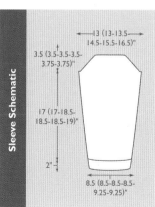

MATERIALS

Main color (M/C): Naturelle DK by
Naturally, shade 251, 8 (8-8-9-10-11)
100 g balls (100% wool).

Color A: Tussock DK by Naturally,
shade 262, 1 100 g ball (85% wool,
15% polyester).

Pair of 4.5 mm needles, 22 in [56 cm]-
long 4.5 mm circular needle (used for
turtleneck), 2 stitch holders, CN, pair of
4 mm dpn for I-cord, large-eyed blunt
sewing needle.

Yarn amounts given are based on average
requirements and are approximate.

TENSION / GAUGE

25 sts and 28 rows = 4 in [10 cm] over
cable pattern.

Take the time to check your gauge;
change needle sizes if necessary to obtain
correct gauge and garment size.

REFER TO TECHNIQUES ON PAGE 12
FOR: I-CORDS.

Symbols Used in This Chart

⊡	p on RS; k on WS	⤬ T6Rrib	
☐	k on RS; p on WS	⤬ T6Lrib	

Chart reads R to L RS rows and L to R WS rows

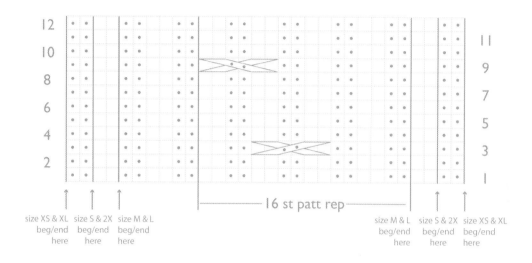

size XS & XL beg/end here size S & 2X beg/end here size M & L beg/end here — 16 st patt rep — size M & L beg/end here size S & 2X beg/end here size XS & XL beg/end here

CABLE PATTERN (16 ST PATT REP ONLY, REFER TO CHART FOR EDGE STS)

Row 1 (RS): (p2, k2) to end.
Row 2: (p2, k2) to end.
Row 3: p2, k2, p2, T6Rrib, p2, k2.
Row 4–8: rep row 2, then rep rows 1 and 2 twice more.
Row 9: (p2, k2) twice, p2, T6Lrib.
Rows 10–12: rep row 2, then rep rows 1 and 2 once more. Rep rows 1–12 for patt.

BACK

Using 4.5 mm needles and M/C, cast on 94 (106-118-134-142-154) sts.

Sizes XS, M, L, and XL work as follows:

RS row: (p2, k2) rep to last 2 sts, p2.

WS row: (k2, p2) rep to last 2 sts, k2.

Sizes S and 2X work as follows:

RS row: (k2, p2) rep to to last 2 sts, k2.

WS row: (p2, k2) rep to last 2 sts p2.

Now following chart, beg/end as indicated for size, place pattern as follows:

RS row: beg at RHS of chart, work first 4 (2-0-0-4-2) sts, then work 16 st patt rep row 1 of chart 5 (6-7-8-8-9) times, 10 (8-6-6-10-8) sts rem, work these as given at LHS of chart.

WS row: beg at LHS of chart,

work first 10 (8-6-6-10-8) sts then work 16 st patt rep row 2 of chart 5 (6-7-8-8-9) times, 4 (2-0-0-4-2) sts rem, work these as given at RHS side of chart.

Cont working chart rows in sequence as set until piece measures 14.5 (15-15-15.75-16.5-16.5) in [37 (38-38-40-42-42) cm] from beg, end with RS row facing for next row.

shape armholes as follows:
Cont working in patt, BO 3 (3-4-4-4-4) sts at beg of next 4 rows, 82 (94-102-118-126-138) sts rem. Work even in patt until armhole measures 7.25 (7.25-7.5-8-8.5-9) in [18.5 (18.5-19-20-21.5-23) cm] from beg of shaping, end with RS row facing for next row.

shape shoulders as follows:

Cont in patt, BO 6 (8-9-12-12-14) sts at beg of next 6 rows. Place rem 46 (46-48-46-54-54) sts on a stitch holder.

FRONT

Work as given for back until armhole measures 4.75 (4.75-5-5.5-5.5-6) in [12 (12-13-14-14-15) cm] from beg of shaping, end with RS row facing for next row.

shape front neck as follows:

Work across 34 (38-40-46-50-54) sts in patt. Turn (this is neck edge). Leave rem 48 (56-62-72-76-84) sts on a spare needle. Cont in patt, dec I st at neck edge on following 16 (14-13-10-14-12) rows, 18 (24-27-36-36-42) sts rem. Work even in patt until armhole measures the same as back before shoulder shaping, end with RS row facing for next row.

shape shoulder as follows:

BO 6 (8-9-12-12-14) sts at beg of next row, work WS row even. Rep the last 2 rows once more. BO rem 6 (8-9-12-12-14) sts.

Return to sts on spare needle. Slip center 14 (18-22-26-26-30) sts onto a stitch holder, rejoin yarn to rem 34 (38-40-46-50-54) sts and work across row. Cont in patt, dec I st at neck edge on following 16 (14-13-10-14-12) rows. Work even in patt until armhole measures the same as back before shoulder shaping,

end with WS row facing for next row.

shape shoulder as follows:

BO 6 (8-9-12-12-14) sts at beg of next row, work RS row even. Rep the last 2 rows once more. BO rem 6 (8-9-12-12-14) sts.

SLEEVE (MAKE 2 ALIKE)

With 4.5 mm needles and Color A, cast on 54 (54-54-54-58-58) sts, work in 2x2 rib as follows:

RS row: (k2, p2) to last 2 sts, k2.

WS row: (p2, k2) to last 2 sts, p2.

Rep last 2 rows. Change to M/C and work a further 10 rows in 2x2 rib as above. Now work in opposite 2x2 rib (forms line for turning back cuff) as follows:

RS row: (p2, k2) to last 2 sts, p2.

WS row: (k2, p2) to last 2 sts, k2.

Rep last 2 rows.

place cable patt as follows:

RS: k0 (0-0-0-2-2), then following row I of chart, work 16 st patt rep 3 times, p2, k2, p2, k0 (0-0-0-2-2).

WS: p0 (0-0-0-2-2), k2, p2, k2, work 16 st patt rep row 2 of chart 3 times, p0 (0-0-0-2-2).

Cont working chart rows in sequence as set, *at the same time* inc every 8th (8-8-6-6-6) row 10 (10-15-12-16-18) times, 74 (74-84-78-90-94) sts, work all inc sts in 2x2 rib throughout. Then

inc every 10th (10-0-8-8-4) row 3 (3-0-6-3-4) times, 80 (80-84-90-96-102) sts. Work even in patt until sleeve measures 17 (17-18.5-18.5-18.5-19) in [43 (43-47-47-47-48) cm] from cuff turn-back line.

shape cap as follows:

Cont in patt BO 3 (3-4-4-4-4) sts at beg of next 4 rows, then dec I st at each end of next 16 (16-16-16-18-18) rows, 36 (36-36-42-44-50) sts rem. Then BO 4 (4-4-5-5-6) sts at beg of next 4 rows. BO rem 20 (20-20-22-24-26) sts.

FINISHING AND TURTLENECK

Weave in ends. Block all pieces to given dimensions. Join both shoulder seams.

Using 4.5 mm circular needle, and M/C beg at LHS shoulder, pick up and knit 18 (20-21-24-28-30) sts down LHS front neck, work in 2x2 rib as set across 14 (18-22-26-26-30) sts from front neck st holder, then pick up and knit 18 (20-21-24-28-30) sts up RHS front neck, then work in 2x2 rib as set across 46 (46-48-46-54-54) sts from back neck st holder, 96 (104-112-120-136-144) sts total.

Working in rnds, work in 2x2 rib as set (size medium only begs and ends p1) work 15 rnds. Then work in opposite 2x2 rib (forms line for turning down neck as at turn-

back for cuff) for a further 14 rnds. Change to Color A and work 4 rows in 2x2 rib as last 14 rnds. BO loosely in rib.

Set in sleeves to armholes. Sew side and sleeve seams, reversing seam for turn-back cuffs. Press lightly, following the instructions on the yarn label.

make and attach I-cords:
Using 4 mm dpns and Color A, make two 3 st I-cords 32 in [81 cm] long and one 3-st I-cord 90 in [229 cm] long.

Thread one of the shorter cords onto a large-eyed blunt sewing needle, use this to attach the cord at the contrast edging of cuff. Thread the cord from WS to RS of cuff (remembering that cuff turns back), bringing it up through a purl section of rib, tie a knot in cord, then thread it back down next purl section of rib to WS. Rep, bringing cord up through each purl section of rib, until you have worked all the way around cuff.

Rep for second cuff.

Rep for collar using longer cord.

mindfulness pointer: don't rush a seed

Pay attention to the first few rows of each piece; they contain the blueprint for the pattern. Without first putting down strong roots, nothing can grow. Remember, you would never rush a seed to come to fruition before it was time. Instead, you take delight in the anticipation of the beauty to come. So don't rush the foundation of your project either. Enjoy watching it miraculously transform before your eyes into a beautiful pattern.

knots and bark

I am a big fan of textures, as you have probably already figured out. Some of my favorites are smooth cotton sheets, dry stone walls, plush teddy bears, and, of course, rugged, gnarled trees. These appeal to both my sense of sight and touch. It fascinates me that you can tell how rough or smooth something is before you actually touch it just by the way that light is reflected from its surface.

We use our senses to enjoy and understand the world. Knitters probably rely most heavily on sight and touch. We use sight in the initial choice of project and yarn, but the feel of the fiber also plays a huge part in its selection. Not only are we going to be touching every inch of the yarn as we make up the garment, but most times it will be touching our skin when the garment is worn.

The textures found on trees can vary greatly. I find pleasure in looking at not only the individual textures, but also how they combine, sometimes within the same tree. This project was born out of the desire to combine several knitted textures in a similar manner. You will find two different cables; one set on choppy reverse stockinette stitch, the other a dense allover pattern. A slip stitch and added crochet cord embroidery add highlights and even more texture.

SIZES / FINISHED CHEST
MEASUREMENTS

XS 33 in [84 cm]

Small 37 in [94 cm]

Medium 41.5 in [105 cm]

Large 44 in [112 cm]

XL 47 in [119 cm]

2X 50.5 in [128 cm]

Instructions are given for smallest size. If changes are necessary for larger sizes, the instructions are given in ( ). Where there is only one set of figures, this applies to all sizes.

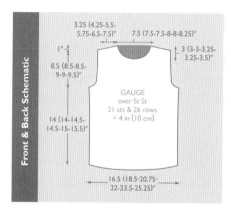

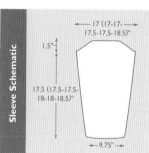

MATERIALS

M/C: Lett-Lopi shade 9427, 8 (9-9-10-11-12) 50 g balls, (100% wool).

Color A: Lett-Lopi shade 0053, 2 (3-3-4-4-4) 50 g balls.

Color B: Lett-Lopi shade 0086, 1 50 g ball.

Pair of 4.5 mm needles, 24 in[61 cm]-long circular 4.5 mm needle (used for turtleneck), 2 stitch holders, CN, 3.5 mm crochet hook, blunt sewing needle.

Yarn amounts given are based on average requirements and are approximate.

TENSION / GAUGE

21 sts and 26 rows = 4 in [10 cm] over stockinette stitch.

Take the time to check your gauge; change needle sizes if necessary to obtain correct gauge and garment size.

REFER TO GLOSSARY ON PAGE 13 FOR: SEED STITCH, AND TO TECHNIQUES ON PAGE 12 FOR WHIPSTITCH.

Symbols Used in This Chart

- ⊡ p on RS; k on WS
- ☐ k on RS; p on WS
- ▨ no stitch
- ⩔ inc2
- ⩘ p3tog
- ⟋ T4L
- ⟋ T5R
- ⟋ C6B
- ⟋ C6F

Chart reads R to L RS rows and L to R WS rows

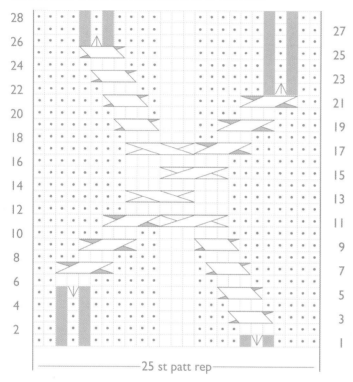

├─────── 25 st patt rep ───────┤

Note: beg 21 sts, inc to 23 sts rows 1–4, inc 25 sts rows 5–21, dec back to 23 sts rows 22–25, dec back to 21 sts rows 26–28

Please see note on placing markers in
Things You Need to Know Before You Begin (p.8)

CABLE PATTERN

Row 1 (RS): p4, inc2 into next st, p4, k3, p9, (23 sts).

Row 2: k9, (p3, k4) twice.

Row 3: p4, T4L, p3, k3, p9.

Row 4: k9, p3, k3, p3, k5.

Row 5: p5, T4L, p2, k3, p6, inc 2 into next st, p2, (25 sts).

Row 6: k2, p3, k6, p3, k2, p3, k6.

Row 7: p6, T4L, p1, k3, p4, T5R, p2.

Row 8: (k4, p3) twice, k1, p3, k7.

Row 9: p7, T4L, k3, p2, T5R, p4.

Row 10: k6, p3, k2, p6, k8.

Row 11: p8, C6B, T5R, p6.

Row 12: k8, p9, k8.

Row 13: p8, k3, C6F, p8.

Row 14: rep row 12.

Row 15: p8, C6B, k3, p8.

Row 16: rep row 12.

Row 17: p6, T5R, C6F, p8.

Row 18: k8, p6, k2, p3, k6.

Row 19: p4, T5R, p2, k3, T4L, p7.

Row 20: k7, p3, k1, (p3, k4) twice.

Row 21: p2, T5R, p4, k3, p1, T4L, p6.

Row 22: k6, p3, k2, p3, k6, p3tog, k2, (23 sts).

Row 23: p9, k3, p2, T4L, p5.

Row 24: k5, p3, k3, p3, k9.

Row 25: p9, k3, p3, T4L, p4.

Row 26: k4, p3tog, k4, p3, k9, (21 sts).

Row 27: p9, k3, p9.

Row 28: k9, p3, k9.

BACK

Using 4.5 mm needles and M/C, cast on 87 (97-109-115-123-133) sts. Work 2 rows in seed st. Work set-up rows as follows:

RS: p25 (28-34-35-39-43), k3, p31 (35-35-39-39-41), k3, p25 (28-34-35-39-43).

WS: k25 (28-34-35-39-43), p3, k31 (35-35-39-39-41), p3, k25 (28-34-35-39-43).

Work these 2 rows, 4 (4-4-4-4-5) more times.

now place cable panel as follows:

Row 1 (RS): p16 (19-25-26-30-34), work row 1 of chart, p13 (17-17-21-21-23), work row 1 of chart, p16 (19-25-26-30-34).

Row 2: k16 (19-25-26-30-34), work row 2 of chart, k13 (17-17-21-21-23), work row 2 of chart, k16 (19-25-26-30-34).

Work rows 3-28 of chart in sequence as now set.

Then work both set-up rows 9 (9-10-10-11-11) times, 18 (18-20-20-22-22) rows total. Now work rows 1-28 of chart, placing as before.

Then work both set-up rows 3 (3-4-4-5-5) times, 6 (6-8-8-10-10) rows total.

Cont working set-up rows throughout.

shape armholes as follows:

BO 3 sts at beg of next 2 rows, then 4 (3-3-4-4-3) sts at beg of following 2 rows, 73 (85-97-101-109-121) sts rem. Work 6 more rows in even patt.

Change to Color A, knit 5 rows (first garter ridge), purl 1 row.

work slip st detail as follows:

RS, using B: sl3 (0-2-1-4-1), *k3, sl2 rep from * to end.

WS, using B: *yf, sl2, yb, k3, rep from * to last 3 (0-2-1-4-1) sts, yf, sl3 (0-2-1-4-1).

Using Color A beg with a knit row work 2 rows in St St, then knit 4 rows (second garter ridge) inc 1 st on last row, 74 (86-98-102-110-122) sts.

now place yoke cable patt as follows:

Row 1 (RS): knit all sts.

Row 2 and all WS rows: purl all sts.

Row 3: k1 (1-1-3-1-1), *C4B, k4, C4F, rep from * to last 1 (1-1-3-1-1) sts, k1 (1-1-3-1-1).

Row 5: knit all sts.

Row 7: k3 (3-3-5-3-3), C4F, C4B, *k4, C4F, C4B, rep from * to last 3 (3-3-5-3-3) sts, k3 (3-3-5-3-3).

Row 8: purl all sts.

Rep rows 1–8 until armhole measures 8.5 (8.5-8.5-9-9-9.5) in [21.5 (21.5-21.5-23-23-24) cm] from beg of shaping.

shape shoulders as follows:

BO 6 (8-10-10-11-13) sts at beg of next 4 rows. BO 5 (7-9-10-12-13) sts at beg of following 2 rows. Leave rem 40 (40-40-42-42-44) sts on a stitch holder.

FRONT

Work as given for back until yoke cable patt has been set.

Rep rows 1–8 yoke cable patt until armhole measures 5.5 (5.5-5.5-5.75-5.75-6) in [14 (14-14-14.5-14.5-15) cm] from beg of shaping, end with RS row facing for next row.

shape front neck as follows:

Cont in patt work across 27 (33-39-40-44-49) sts, turn (this is neck edge). Leave rem 47 (53-59-62-66-73) sts on a spare needle.

Dec 1 st at neck edge of next 4 rows, then every following RS row 6 times, 17 (23-29-30-34-39) sts rem. Work even until armhole measures same as back before shoulder shaping, end with RS row facing for next row.

shape shoulder as follows:

BO 6 (8-10-10-11-13) sts at beg of next row. Work WS row even. Rep last 2 rows once more. BO rem 5 (7-9-10-12-13) sts.

Return to sts on spare needle. Slip center 20 (20-20-22-22-24) sts onto a stitch holder. Rejoin yarn and work to end.

Dec 1 st at neck edge of next 4 rows, then every following RS row 6 times, 17 (23-29-30-34-39) sts rem. Work even until armhole measures same as back before shoulder shaping, end WS row facing for next row.

shape shoulder as follows:
BO 6 (8-10-10-11-13) sts at beg of next row. Work RS row even. Rep last 2 rows once more. BO rem 5 (7-9-10-12-13) sts.

SLEEVE (MAKE 2 ALIKE)

Using 4.5 mm needles and M/C, cast on 51 sts. Work 2 rows in seed st.

Work set-up rows as follows:

RS: p24, k3, p24.

WS: k24, p3, k24.

Work these 2 rows, once more (4 rows total).

place cable panel as follows:

Row 1(RS): p15, work row 1 of chart, p15.

Row 2: k15, work row 2 of chart, k15.

Work rows 3–28 of chart in sequence as now set, then cont working set-up rows as above throughout, *at the same time* inc 1 st at each end of row 5 and every following 4th row 7 (7-7-8-8-10) times, 67 (67-67-69-69-73) sts, work all inc sts in rev St St throughout. Then inc I st at each end of every following 6th row 12 times, 91 (91-91-93-93-97) sts. Work even until sleeve measures 17.5 (17.5-17.5-18-18-18.5) in [44.5 (44.5-44.5-45.5-45.5-47) cm] from beg.

shape cap as follows:

Cont in patt as set BO 3 sts at beg of next 2 rows. Then BO 3 (3-3-4-4-3) sts at beg of following 2 rows, 79 (79-79-79-79-85) sts rem. BO 9 (9-9-9-9-10) sts at beg of following 6 rows. BO rem 25 sts.

TURTLENECK AND FINISHING

Weave in all ends. Block all pieces to given dimensions. Sew both shoulder seams.

first neckline:

Using circular 4.5 mm needle and Color A, with RS facing beg at CF (center of sts on holder) knit across 10 (10-10-11-11-12)

sts from front neck st holder, pick up and knit 15 (19-23-25-27-29) sts up RHS front neck, knit across 40 (40-40-42-42-44) sts from back neck st holder, pick up and knit 15 (19-23-25-27-29) sts down LHS front neck, then knit across rem 10 (10-10-11-11-12) sts from front neck st holder, 90 (98-106-114-118-126) sts total.

Work back and forth as follows:

WS row: k3, purl to last 3 sts, k3.

RS row: knit all sts.

Rep the last 2 rows 3 times more. Knit 3 rows. BO all sts knitwise.

second neckline:

Using circular 4.5 mm needle and Color B, beg at left shoulder seam, with WS facing pick up and knit the same number of sts as for first neckline. Working in rnds, knit 11 rnds (forms St St). Purl 1 rnd, knit 1 rnd, rep last 2 rnds once more, (forms garter ridges). Knit 6 rnds. BO all sts knitwise.

Using 3.5 mm crochet hook and Color B, make the following cords, working in chain st:

Four 48 in [122 cm] long (approx 230 chains).

One 26 in [66 cm] long (approx 120 chains).

Thread one of the longer cords onto a blunt sewing needle and whipstitch over 1st garter ridge below slipstitch detail on back, forming diagonals. Repeat with 2nd cord over 2nd garter ridge above slipstitch detail. Repeat for both garter ridges on front, using the rem 2 long cords.

Thread shorter cord onto blunt sewing needle and lace across CF opening on first neckline, forming an X and leaving ends hanging loosely to RS of neckline.

Set in sleeves to armholes. Sew side and sleeve seams. Press lightly, following the instructions on the yarn label.

mindfulness pointer: get in touch

How well developed is your sense of touch? Can you feel a change in the pattern as the piece slides through your hands, before you even see it? Try closing your eyes and find out if you can knit by feel alone. Just imagine all the things you can do if you hone this skill: chat with friends or watch your favorite TV program while knitting. If you are not an experienced knitter, try this on the simple sections of the pattern.

inspired by your surroundings

Traditional Aran sweater patterns incorporated cables to depict the ropes used by the fishermen who wore these sweaters. So as I thought about an update to the traditional cabled sweater, I wondered which surroundings I could draw on for inspiration that are a part of our daily lives.

This is when I began noticing the cable-like patterns in tree bark. I was drawn to the tactile nature of the bumps and hollows, as I imagine many people are. But rather than the simple repetition of twists, these cables meandered, and showed little repetition. The regularity of rope twists condenses easily into repeat patterns, whereas the organic refuses to conform to this structure, which is in fact its beauty.

To address this, I designed two cables for this project whose repeats are not easily detected. Both have long row repeats and are not divisible by each other, so they are almost always offset, eliminating any true horizontal breaks. The cable used in the center panels is asymmetrical, leaving areas of reverse stockinette stitch. This allows each cable to infringe on its neighbor, making it difficult to see the vertical breaks.

SIZES / FINISHED CHEST
MEASUREMENTS

Small 42 in [106.5 cm]

Medium 46 in [117 cm]

Large 50 in [127 cm]

XL 54 in [137 cm]

Instructions are given for smallest size. If changes are necessary for larger sizes, the instructions are given in ( ). Where there is only one set of figures, this applies to all sizes.

*A full-length photograph of this sweater can be found on page 75.

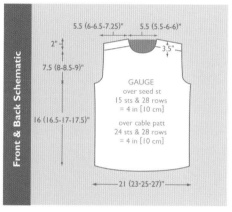

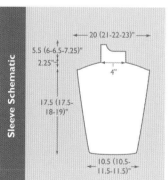

Skye Tweed by Classic Elite Yarns (100% wool).

Main Color: shade 1272, 16 (16-18-20) 50 g balls.

Color A: shade 1291, 1 50 g ball.

Pair of 4.5 mm needles, circular (22ins [56 cms] long) 4.5 mm needle (used for neckband), 5 mm needle (used for neckband BO), 8 stitch holders, CN.

Yarn amounts given are based on average requirements and are approximate.

TENSION / GAUGE

15 sts and 28 rows = 4 in [10 cm] over seed st.

24 sts and 28 rows = 4 in [10 cm] over cable pattern.

98 sts for center panel (back and front) measures 16 in [40.5 cm] in width.

Take the time to check your gauge; change needle sizes if necessary to obtain correct gauge and garment size.

REFER TO GLOSSARY ON PAGE 13 FOR: SEED STITCH AND TO TECHNIQUES ON PAGE 12 FOR SHORT ROWS, 3-NEEDLE BIND OFF.

Symbols Used in These Charts

⊡ p on RS; k on WS	⧄ T3B ⧄ C4B ⧄ T4B
☐ k on RS; p on WS	⧅ T3F ⧅ C4F ⧅ T4F

Chart A

Chart reads R to L RS rows and L to R WS rows

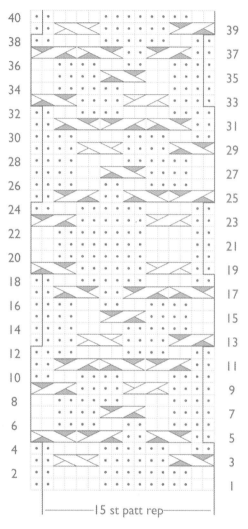

└─ 15 st patt rep ─┘

Chart B

Chart reads R to L RS rows and L to R WS rows

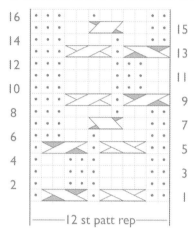

└─ 12 st patt rep ─┘

Please see note on placing markers in
Things You Need to Know Before You Begin (p.8)

PATTERN A (15 ST PATT REP IS * TO *)

Row 1 (RS): *k2, p8, k4, p1*, p1.

Row 2: k1, *k1, p4, k8, p2*.

Row 3: *T4F, p6, C4F, p1*, p1.

Row 4: k1, *k1, p4, k6, p2, k2*.

Row 5: p1, *p1, T4F, p2, T4B, T4F*.

Row 6: *p2, k4, p2, k2, p2, k3*, k1.

Row 7: p1, *p3, k2, T4B, p4, k2*.

Row 8: *p2, k6, p4, k3*, k1.

Row 9: p1, *p3, C4B, p4, T4B*.

Row 10: *k2, p2, k4, p4, k3*, k1.

Row 11: p1, *p1, T4B, T4F, T4B, p2*.

Row 12: *k4, p4, k4, p2, k1*, k1.

Row 13: .*T4B, p4, C4F, p3*, p1.

Row 14: k1, *k3, p4, k6, p2*.

Row 15: *k2, p4, T4B, k2, p3*, p1.

Row 16: k1, *k3, p2, k2, p2, k4, p2*.

Row 17: *T4F, T4B, p2, T4F, p1*, p1.

Row 18: k1, *k1, p2, k6, p4, k2*.

Row 19: p1, *p1, C4B, p6, T4F*.

Row 20: *p2, k8, p4, k1*, k1.

Row 21: p1, *p1, k4, p8, k2*.

Row 22: rep row 20.

Row 23: p1, *p1, C4B, p6, T4B*.

Row 24: *k2, p2, k6, p4, k1*, k1.

Row 25: *T4B, T4F, p2, T4B, p1*, p1.

Row 26: k1, *k3, p2, k2, p2, k4, p2*.

Row 27: *k2, p4, T4F, k2, p3*, p1.

Row 28: k1, *k3, p4, k6, p2*.

Row 29: *T4F, p4, C4F, p3*, p1.

Row 30: k1, *k3, p4, k4, p2, k2*.

Row 31: *p2, T4F, T4B, T4F, p1*, p1.

Row 32: k1, *k1, p2, k4, p4, k4*.

Row 33: p1, *p3, C4B, p4, T4F*.

Row 34: *p2, k6, p4, k3*, k1.

Row 35: p1, *p3, k2, T4F, p4, k2*.

Row 36: *p2, k4, p2, k2, p2, k3*, k1.

Row 37: p1, *p1, T4B, p2, T4F, T4B*.

Row 38: *k2, p4, k6, p2, k1*, k1.

Row 39: *T4B, p6, C4F, p1*, p1.

Row 40: rep row 2.

Rep rows 1–40 for patt A.

PATTERN B

Row 1 (RS): p2, C4F, p1, T4F, p1.

Row 2: k1, p2, k3, p4, k2.

Row 3: p2, k4, p3, k2, p1.

Row 4: rep row 2.

Row 5: p2, C4F, p1, T4B, p1.

Row 6: k3, p2, k1, p4, k2.

Row 7: p2, k2, T3F, k2, p3.

Row 8: k3, p4, k1, p2, k2.

Row 9: T4B, p1, C4B, p3.

Row 10: k3, p4, k3, p2.

Row 11: k2, p3, k4, p3.

Row 12: rep row 10.

Row 13: T4F, p1, C4B, p3.

Row 14: k3, p4, k1, p2, k2.

Row 15: p2, k2, T3B, k2, p3.

Row 16: k3, p2, k1, p4, k2.

Rep rows 1–6 for patt B.

BACK

Using M/C and 4.5 mm needles, cast on 116 (124-132-140) sts.

Work set-up rows as follows:

RS row: work 9 (13-17-21) sts in seed st, p1, (p2, k4, p1, k2, p3) twice, p1, (work 15 st patt rep row 1 Chart A) 3 times, p2, (p2, k4, p1, k2, p3) twice, p1, work 9 (13-17-21) sts in seed st.

WS row: work 9 (13-17-21) sts in seed st, k1, (k3, p2, k1, p4, k2) twice, k2, (work 15 st patt rep row 2 Chart A) 3 times, k1, (k3, p2, k1, p4, k2) twice, k1, work 9 (13-17-21) sts in seed st.

Repeat these 2 rows twice more (repeating rows 1 and 2 Chart A) 6 rows total.

place cable panels as follows:

Row 1: work 9 (13-17-21) sts in seed st, p1, (work 12 st patt rep row 1 Chart B) twice, p1, (work 15 st patt rep row 1 Chart A) 3 times, p2, (work 12 st patt rep row 1 Chart B) twice, p1, work 9 (13-17-21) sts in seed st.

Row 2: work 9 (13-17-21) sts in seed st, k1, (work 12 st patt rep row 2 Chart B) twice, k2, (work 15 st patt rep row 2 Chart A) 3 times, k1, (work 12 st patt rep row 2 Chart B) twice, k1, work 9 (13-17-21) sts in seed st.

Cont working in cable panels as now set, working rows given for both charts in sequence. *Note:* chart row reps do not coincide, and additional st given in Chart A moves from LHS to RHS as indicated.

Work as set until back measures 16 (16.5-17-17.5) in [40.5 (42-43-44.5) cm] from beg, end with RS row facing for next row.

shape armholes as follows:
Cont in patt BO 3 sts at beg of next 2 rows, then 2 sts at beg of following 2 rows. Dec 1 st at each end of following next 3 RS rows, 100 (108-116-124) sts rem. Work even in patt until armhole measures 7.5 (8-8.5-9) in [19 (20-21.5-23) cm] from beg of shaping, end RS row facing for next row.

shape shoulders as follows:
Cont in patt work to last 11 (12-13-15) sts, wrap next st, turn, leave rem sts unworked in hold.

Work WS to last 11 (12-13-15) sts, wrap next st, turn.

Next RS row: work to last 22 (24-26-30) sts, wrap next st, turn. Rep for WS row.

Next RS row: work to last 33 (37-40-44) sts, wrap next st, turn. Rep for WS row.

Leave each set of 33 (37-40-44) sts for saddle shoulders on separate stitch holders. Leave rem 34

(34-36-36) sts at center back on another stitch holder.

FRONT

Work as given for back until piece measures 6.5 (7-7.5-8) in [16.5 (18-19-20) cm] from beg of armhole shaping, end RS row facing for next row.

shape shoulders and front neck as follows:
Cont in patt work across 39 (43-46-50) sts, turn (this is neck edge). Leave rem 61 (65-70-74) sts on a spare needle.

Dec 1 st at neck edge on next 6 rows, 33 (37-40-44) sts rem.

Work next row (WS) to last 11 (12-13-15) sts, wrap next st, turn, leave rem sts unworked in hold. Work RS row even in patt.

Next WS row: work to last 22 (24-26-30) sts, wrap next st, turn.

Work RS row even in patt.

Leave these 33 (37-40-44) sts for LH saddle shoulder on a stitch holder.

Return to sts on spare needle. Slip center 22 (22-24-24) sts onto a stitch holder, rejoin yarn and work to end in patt.

Dec 1 st at neck edge on next 6 rows, 33 (37-40-44) sts rem.

Work WS row even in patt.

Work RS row to last 11 (12-13-15) sts, wrap next st, turn, leave rem sts unworked in hold. Work WS row even in patt.

Next RS row: work to last 22 (24-26-30) sts, wrap next st, turn. Work WS row even in patt.

Leave these 33 (37-40-44) sts for RH saddle shoulder on a stitch holder.

SLEEVE (MAKE 2 ALIKE)

Using Color A and 4.5 mm needles, cast on 48 (48-52-52) sts, beg with a knit row, work 7 rows in St St.

Change to M/C and purl 1 row, inc 4 sts evenly across row, 52 (52-56-56) sts.

Work set-up rows as follows:

RS row: work 13 (13-15-15) sts in seed st, p1, (p2, k4, p1, k2, p3) twice, p1, work 13 (13-15-15) sts in seed st.

WS row: work 13 (13-15-15) sts in seed st, k1, (k3, p2, k1, p4, k2) twice, k1, work 13 (13-15-15) sts in seed st.

place cable panels as follows:
Row 1: work 13 (13-15-15) sts in seed st, p1, (work 12 st patt rep row 1 Chart B) twice, p1, work 13 (13-15-15) sts in seed st.

Row 2: work 13 (13-15-15) sts in seed st, k1, (work 12 st patt rep row 2 Chart B) twice, k1, work 13 (13-15-15) sts in seed st.

Cont working in cable panels as now set, working rows given for chart in sequence, *at the same time* inc 1 st at each end of row 7 then every following 6th row 17 (13-15-15) times, 88 (80-88-88) sts.

Then inc 1 st at each end of every following 0th (4-4-4) rows 0 (6-4-6) times, 88 (92-96-100) sts. Work all inc sts in seed st. Work even until sleeve measures 17.5 (17.5-18-19) in [44.5 (44.5-46-48) cm] from beg of cable panels.

shape top as follows:

Cont in patt as set BO 3 sts at beg of next 2 rows, then 2 sts at beg of following 2 rows. Then dec 1 st at each end of next 10 rows, 58 (62-66-70) sts rem. BO 15 (17-19-21) at beg of next 2 rows, 28 sts rem.

work saddle extension as follows:

Work on the 28 sts in patt until piece measures 5.5 (6-6.5-7.25) in [14 (15-16.5-18.5) cm] from last BO.

shape neckline at top of sleeve

For LH sleeve, end with RS row facing for next row.

Work across 8 sts, turn, leave rem 20 sts on a stitch holder.

WS row: p2tog, work to end.

RS row: work to last 2 sts, k2tog.

Rep the last 2 rows once more, plus WS row again.

P3tog, break off yarn and draw through loop.

For RH sleeve, end with WS row facing for next row.

Work across 8 sts, turn, leave rem 20 sts on a stitch holder.

RS row: k2tog, work to end.

WS row: work to last 2 sts, p2tog.

Rep the last 2 rows once more, plus RS row again.

K3tog, break off yarn and draw through loop.

FINISHING

Weave in ends. Block all pieces to given dimensions.

Join saddle shoulder seams as follows: using Color A and 4.5 mm needles for both stages a and b below.

a) with RS facing pick up at knit 33 (37-40-44) sts along front shoulder edge of RH sleeve saddle extension.

b) with RS facing knit across 33 (37-40-44) sts from front RH shoulder stitch holder.

With both needles from stages a and b pointing in same direction, work 3-needle BO, using Color A, creating a ridge on RS. Rep

for second front shoulder. Rep for both back shoulders.

Using circular 4.5 mm needle and M/C, with RS facing and beg at RHS back saddle seam, work across 34 (34-36-36) sts from back neck stitch holder in seed st, pick up and knit 3 sts from LH back sleeve, work across 20 sts from LH sleeve stitch holder in seed st, pick up and knit 5 sts down LHS front neck, work across 22 (22-24-24) sts from front neck stitch holder in seed st, pick up and knit 5 sts up RHS front neck, work across 20 sts from RH sleeve stitch holder in seed st, pick up and knit 3 sts from RH back sleeve, 112 (112-116-116) sts. Join in rnd, placing a marker at first st.

Work 4 rnds in seed st.

Change to A and knit 10 rnds (forms St St). BO using 5 mm needle. Allow last 10 rnds to roll to RS and lightly tack in place at front saddle seams.

Set sleeves into armholes. Join side and sleeve seams. Lightly tack roll at lower edges of sleeves at seam. Press lightly, following the instructions on the yarn label.

mindfulness pointer: growing through challenges

When we knit cables, we are used to seeing instructions with simple, short repeats that we can easily memorize. So when you look at the charts for this project, they may appear a little daunting at first, but truly there is a pattern to each. I have to admit that the repetitions are too long to be easily memorized, so don't try to. Take it each row at a time and allow yourself to enjoy the challenge of feeling your way organically through each piece. Remember, your expertise will only grow if you attempt a challenge.

order and chaos

In Helen Humphreys's novel *The Lost Garden*, the main character, a gardener, describes how, when working in a formal garden, she tries to create order out of the chaos of nature. If the garden is untended for too long, the well-manicured beds will succumb once again to the chaos. When designing a knitted garment, there needs to be an underlying order and repetition to the pattern. If not, every row would be different, and the instructions for an average sweater would become two hundred lines of directions or charts.

So in much the same way as a gardener brings order to the chaos of nature, when I began using nature (tree bark in particular) as my inspiration, I had to find ways of taming the unruly power while still allowing the organic beauty to shine through.

I selected cables that use odd numbers, by their very nature not balanced and equal. Then, by joining two together, they become even, symmetrical, and more grounded. By incorporating both, and switching between odd and even numbered patterns, I manage to bring an organic, almost random, feel while still maintaining order and repetition. This produces a tension between two poles, just as we find in a garden, where the order feels like it is on the point of returning to its natural state of chaos.

SIZES / FINISHED CHEST
MEASUREMENTS
Small 42 in [106 cm]
Medium 48 in [122 cm]
Large 54 in [137 cm]
XL 60 in [152 cm]

Instructions are given for smallest size. If changes are necessary for larger sizes, the instructions are given in ( ). Where there is only one set of figures, this applies to all sizes.

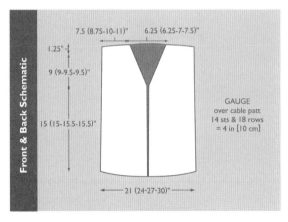

Front & Back Schematic

7.5 (8.75-10-11)"   6.25 (6.25-7-7.5)"

1.25"

9 (9-9.5-9.5)"

15 (15-15.5-15.5)"

21 (24-27-30)"

GAUGE
over cable patt
14 sts & 18 rows
= 4 in [10 cm]

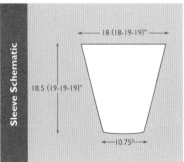

Sleeve Schematic

18 (18-19-19)"

18.5 (19-19-19)"

10.75"

MATERIALS

Van Dyck by Needful Yarns, shade 130,
10 (11-12-13) 100 g balls.

Pair of 6.5 mm needles, 36 in [91 cm]-
long circular 6.5 mm needle (used for
collar), CN.

Yarn amounts given are based on average
requirements and are approximate.

TENSION / GAUGE

14 sts and 18 rows = 4 in [10 cm] over
cable pattern.

Take the time to check your gauge;
change needle sizes if necessary to obtain
correct gauge and garment size.

REFER TO GLOSSARY ON PAGE 13 FOR:
SEED STITCH.

Symbols Used in This Chart

- ⊡ p on RS; k on WS
- ☐ k on RS; p on WS
- ⟨⟩ C2F
- ⟨⟩ T2B
- ⟨⟩ T2F
- ⟨⟩ T3B
- ⟨⟩ T3F
- ⟨⟩ C4B

Chart reads R to L RS rows and L to R WS rows

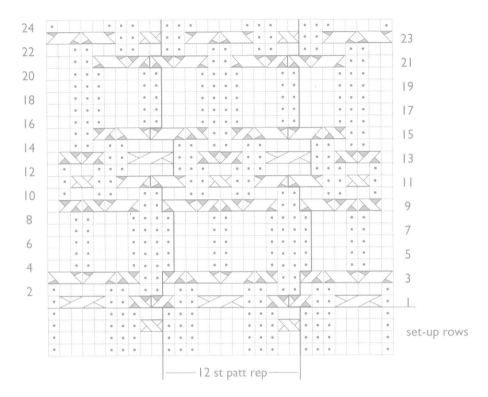

set-up rows

12 st patt rep

CABLE PATTERN

Set-up rows

1st row (RS): p1, k4, p3, *k2, p3, k4, p3, rep from * to last 10 sts, k2, p3, k4, p1.

2nd row: k1, p4, k3, p2, * k3, p4, k3, p2, rep from * to last 8 sts, k3, p4, k1.

3rd row: p1, k4, p3, *C2F, p3, k4, p3, rep from * to last 10 sts, C2F, p3, k4, p1.

4th row: as previous WS row.

Row 1 (RS): p1, C4B, p2, T2B, *T2F, p2, C4B, p2, T2B, rep from * to last 9 sts, T2F, p2, C4B, p1.

Row 2: k1, p4, k2, p1, k2, *p1, k2, p4, k2, p1, k2, rep from *

to last 8 sts, p1, k2, p4, k1.

Row 3: T3B, T3F, T2B, *p2, T2F, T3B, T3F, T2B, rep from * to last 10 sts, p2, T2F, T3B, T3F.

Row 4: p2, k2, p3, k4, *p3, k2, p3, k4, rep from * to last 7 sts, p3, k2, p2.

Row 5: k2, p2, k3, *p4, k3, p2, k3, rep from * to last 11 sts, p4, k3, p2, k2.

Rows 6–8: rep rows 4 and 5, then row 4 once more.

Row 9: k1, T2F, T2B, T3F, *p2, T3B, T2F, T2B, T3F, rep from * to last 10 sts, p2, T3B, T2F, T2B, k1.

Row 10: p1, k1, p2, (k2, p2) to last 2 sts, k1, p1.

Row 11: k1, p1, C2F, p2, T3F, *T3B, p2, C2F, p2, T3F, rep from * to last 9 sts, T3B, p2, C2F, p1, k1.

Row 12: p1, k1, p2, k3, p4, *k3, p2, k3, p4, rep from * to last 7 sts, k3, p2, k1, p1.

Row 13: k1, T2B, T2F, p2, *C4B, p2, T2B, T2F, p2, rep from * to last 11 sts C4B, p2, T2B, T2F, k1.

Row 14: p2, k2, p1, k2, p4, *(k2, p1) twice, k2, p4, rep from * to last 7 sts, k2, p1, k2, p2.

Row 15: k2, p2, T2F, T3B, *T3F, T2B, p2, T2F, T3B, rep from *, to last 9 sts, T3F, T2B, p2, k2.

Row 16: p2, k3, p3, k2, *p3, k4, p3, k2, rep from * to last 8 sts, p3, k3, p2.

Row 17: k2, p3, k3, *p2, k3, p4, k3, rep from * to last 10 sts, p2, k3, p3, k2.

Rows 18–20: rep rows 16 and 17, then row 16 once more.

Row 21: k2, p2, T3B, T2F, *T2B, T3F, p2, T3B, T2F, rep from * to last 9 sts, T2B, T3F, p2, k2.

Row 22: (p2, k2) to last 2 sts, p2.

Row 23: T3F, T3B, p2, *C2F, p2, T3F, T3B, p2, rep from * to last 10 sts, C2F, p2, T3F, T3B.

Row 24: k1, p4, k3, p2, *k3, p4, k3, p2, rep from * to last 8 sts, k3, p4, k1.

Rep rows 1–24 for patt.

BACK

Using 6.5 mm needles, cast on 74 (84-94-104) sts, work 1 row in seed st.

place pattern as follows:

RS (following instructions given for 1st set-up row): p4 (3-2-7), beg at RHS of chart work first 8 sts, then work 12 st patt rep 4 (5-6-6) times, 14 (13-12-17) sts rem, work as given last 10 sts at LHS of chart, p4 (3-2-7).

WS (following instructions given for 2nd set-up row): k4 (3-2-7), beg at LHS of chart work first 10 sts, then work 12 st patt rep 4 (5-6-6) times, 12 (11-10-15) sts rem, work as given last 8 sts at RHS of chart, k4 (3-2-7).

Work next 2 rows in patt as set, following instructions given for 3rd and 4th set-up rows.

Cont working chart rows 1–24 (only) in sequence as set, until piece measures 24 (24-25-25) in [61 (61-63.5-63.5) cm].

shape shoulders as follows:

BO 8 (11-11-13) sts at beg of next 2 rows. Then BO 9 (10-12-13) sts at beg of following 4 rows. Leave rem 22 (22-24-26) sts on a stitch holder.

RH FRONT

Using 6.5 mm needles, cast on 35 (40-45-50) sts, work 1 row in seed st.

place pattern as follows:

Work all 30 sts from chart.

RS: p1 (7-13-13), work 1st set-up row of chart, p4 (3-2-7).

WS: k4 (3-2-7), work 2nd set-up row of chart, k1 (7-13-13).

RS: p1 (7-13-13), work 3rd set-up row of chart, p4 (3-2-7).

WS: k4 (3-2-7), work 4th set-up row of chart, k1 (7-13-13).

Now cont working chart rows 1–24 (only) in sequence as set until piece measures 15 (15-14.5-14) in [38 (38-37-35.5) cm], end RS row facing for next row.

shape neck as follows:

RS: p1 (5-11-11), p2tog, work in patt to end. Work 5 rows even in patt.

Next row: p1 (4-10-10), p2tog, work in patt to end. Work 5 rows even in patt.

Next row: p1 (3-9-9), p2tog, work in patt to end. Work 3 rows even in patt.

Next row: p1 (2-8-8), p2tog, work in patt to end. Work 3 rows even in patt.

Next row: p1 (1-7-7), p2tog, work in patt to end. Work 3 rows even in patt.

S and M sizes: rep last 4 rows 4 more times.

L and XL sizes: cont rep last 4 rows 5 (6) more times, working 1 less st before the p2tog on each dec row as before.

All sizes: 26 (31-35-39) sts rem, work even in patt until piece measures the same as back before shoulder shaping, end WS row facing for next row.

shape shoulder as follows:

BO 8 (11-11-13) sts at beg of next row. Work RS row even. Then BO 9 (10-12-13) sts at beg of next row. Work RS row even. BO rem 9 (10-12-13) sts.

LH FRONT

Using 6.5 mm needles, cast on 35 (40-45-50) sts, work 1 row in seed st.

place pattern as follows:

Work all 30 sts from chart.

RS: p4 (3-2-7), work 1st set-up row of chart, p1 (7-13-13).

WS: k1 (7-13-13), work 2nd set-up row of chart, k4 (3-2-7).

RS: p4 (3-2-7), work 3rd set-up row of chart, p1 (7-13-13).

WS: k1 (7-13-13), work 4th set-up row of chart, k4 (3-2-7).

Cont working chart rows 1-24 (only) in sequence as set until piece measures 15 (15-14.5-14) in [38 (38-37-35.5) cm], end WS row facing for next row.

shape neck as follows:

WS: k1 (5-11-11), k2tog, work in patt to end. Work 5 rows even in patt.

Next row: k1 (4-10-10), k2tog, work in patt to end. Work 5 rows even in patt.

Next row: k1 (3-9-9), k2tog, work in patt to end. Work 3 rows even in patt.

Next row: k1 (2-8-8), k2tog, work in patt to end. Work 3 rows even in patt.

Next row: k1 (1-7-7), k2tog, work in patt to end. Work 3 rows even in patt.

S and M sizes: rep last 4 rows 4 more times.

L and XL sizes: Cont rep last 4 rows 5 (6) more times, working 1 less st before the k2tog on each dec row as before.

All sizes: 26 (31-35-39) sts rem, work even in patt until piece measures the same as back before shoulder shaping, end RS row facing for next row.

shape shoulder as follows:

BO 8 (11-11-13) sts at beg of next row. Work WS row even. Then BO 9 (10-12-13) sts at beg of next row. Work WS row even. BO rem 9 (10-12-13) sts.

SLEEVE (MAKE 2 ALIKE)

Using 6.5 mm needles cast on 38 sts, work 1 row seed st.

Place pattern as follows: work all 30 sts from chart.

RS: p4, work 1st set-up row of chart, p4.

WS: k4, work 2nd set-up row of chart, k4.

RS: p4, work 3rd set-up row of chart, p4.

WS: k4, work 4th set-up row of chart, k4.

Now cont working chart rows 1–24 (only) in sequence as set, *at the same time* inc 1 st at each end of row 1 and every following 4th row 0 (0-2-2) times, 40 (40-44-44) sts on needle. Work all inc sts in rev St St throughout. Then inc 1 st at each end of every following

6th row 12 (12-11-11) times, 64 (64-66-66) sts. Work even until piece measures 18.5 (19-19-19) in [47 (48-48-48) cm]. BO all sts loosely.

COLLAR AND FINISHING

Weave in ends. Block all pieces to given dimensions.

Join both shoulder seams.

Using 6.5 mm circular needle, with RS facing and beg at lower edge of RHS front, pick up and knit 114 (114-116-115) sts up side RHS front, knit across 22 (22-24-26) sts from back neck st holder, dec 1 (1-0-0) st at CB, then pick up and knit 114 (114-116-115) sts down LHS front, 249 (249-256-256) sts total.

Work back and forth as follows:

RS: k1, p3, (k3, p4) to last 7 sts, k3, p3, k1.

WS: (k4, p3) to last 4 sts, k4.

Rep these 2 rows 6 more times (14 rows total). BO loosely in patt.

Set in sleeves to armholes. Sew side and sleeve seams.

Press lightly, following the instructions on the yarn label.

mindfulness pointer: the rhythm of the seasons

Consider how each part of the pattern feels: which parts feel like order and which chaos? Does the last row of a repeat feel like you are coming full circle, only to begin the process all over again, just as a gardener might when planting bulbs or raking up leaves each year? Does the purl row feel like the dormancy of winter, a necessary fallowness in order to have the beauty of the spring that will follow?

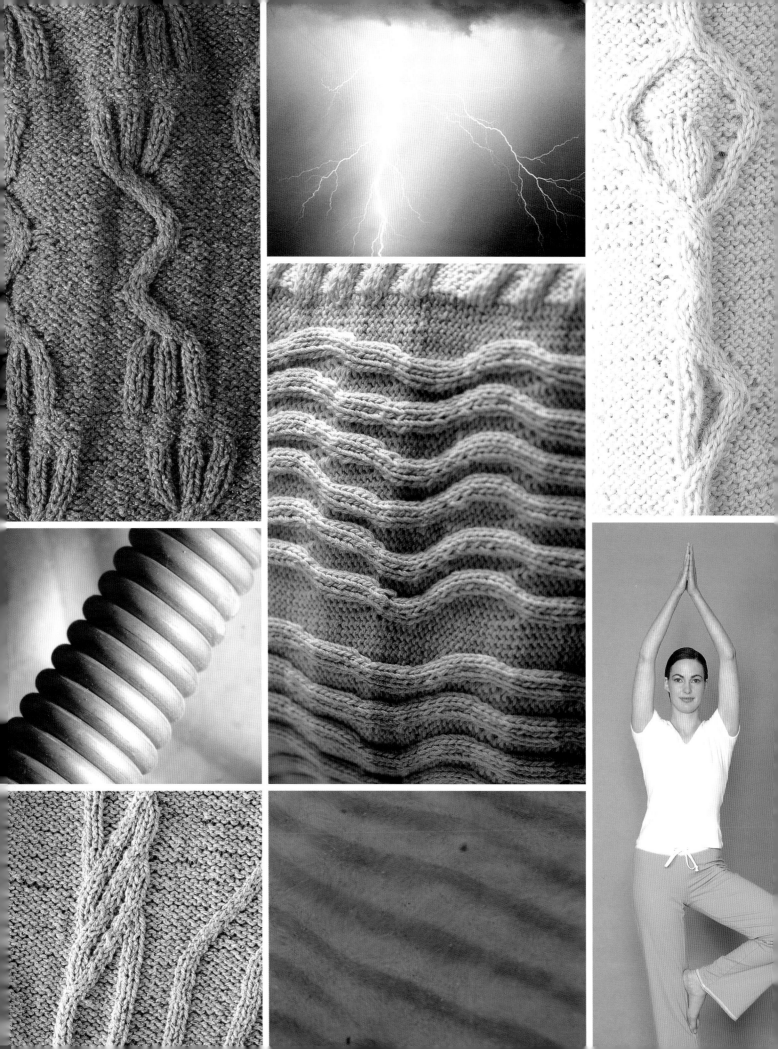

inspired by energy

THE GRAPHIC DEPICTION OF ENERGY FORCES OR OF THE SHAPES FORMED BY THE BODY WHILE PRACTICING YOGA CAN INSPIRE CABLE PATTERNS, AND ALSO OFFER A FOCUS FOR CONTEMPLATION DURING THE KNITTING PROCESS.

Sometimes, the most fascinating sources of inspiration are not those that we seek, but those that we happen upon, serendipitously, in our daily lives. When we are closely attuned to our surroundings, ordinary events can affect and inspire us in surprising ways.

Science teaches us that energy can never be created or destroyed—it can only be changed. Energy is everywhere and takes many varied forms. Whether we are aware of the energy forces within us or around us, they are constantly at play and are an ever-changing phenomenon.

I have learned to become more aware of the energies that exist in the body through my yoga practice. As a result of this awareness, I became interested in the ways scholars since ancient times have sought to depict these forces. I discovered that even though they might have begun at different points, they had come up with very similar ways of describing the energy centers within the body.

I drew on all these ideas when designing the projects for this chapter. The diversity of the source material has consequently given rise to a wide range of approaches, but each is still connected to the others through the underlying notion of depicting energy forces.

tree-pose yoga bag

Yoga practice has many facets. I unexpectedly discovered that the sensation of energy pathways in the body had particular resonance for me. Once the body is properly aligned, energy flows more easily. This flow can be gained physically when practicing yoga, or mentally by cleansing the mind of distraction.

When the mind is quieted, distractions and technical limitations no longer overpower the creative process. Ideas flow smoothly and abundantly.

One day, I caught a glimpse of myself in the mirror while practicing the tree pose. My alignment must have been pretty good because as I saw my reflection, I thought, "I could knit this pose." At the time, I was in the process of looking at trees for inspiration; I hadn't expected to find my inspiration indoors.

At that moment, I felt my foot sending down roots into the earth, tapping directly into the energy that Mother Nature stores there and drawing it up through my body before releasing it to the heavens through the crown of my head. I truly felt like a conduit for that energy. I know that when I allowed myself to think about knitting, I had interrupted the flow, but as compensation I had been given a gift of insight. Still, I resolved to practice a little more mindfully next time.

FINISHED SIZE
Bag will measure 26.5 in [67 cm] long and 14 in [35.5 cm] in circumference.

MATERIALS

Hemp Yarn from Infiknit, shade Natural, 3 4 oz balls.

Pair of 3.5 mm needles, pair of 3.5 mm dpns, CN, cardboard to make inner base.

Yarn amount given is based on average requirements and is approximate.

TENSION / GAUGE
24 sts and 28 rows = 4 in [10 cm] over stockinette stitch.

Take the time to check your gauge; change needle sizes if necessary to obtain correct gauge and garment size.

REFER TO GLOSSARY ON PAGE 13 FOR: SEED STITCH, AND TO TECHNIQUES ON PAGE 12 FOR: SHORT ROWS, I-CORDS.

Symbols Used in This Chart

[•] p on RS; k on WS   C3B   C4B   C5B

[ ] k on RS; p on WS   C3F   C4F   C5F

   T3B   T4B   T5R

   T3F   T4F   T5L

Chart reads R to L RS rows and L to R WS rows

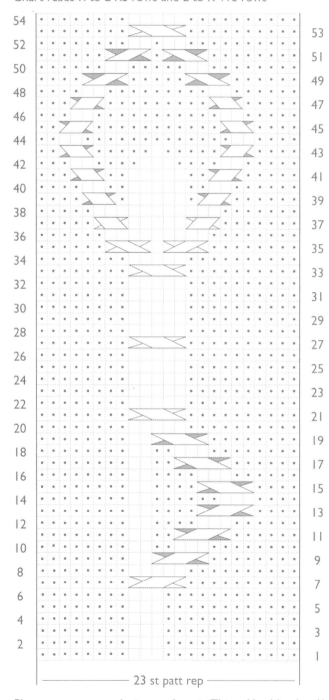

23 st patt rep

Please see note on placing markers in Things You Need to Know Before You Begin (p.8)

CABLE PATTERN

Row 1 (RS): p12, k3, p8.

Row 2: k8, p3, k12.

Rows 3–6: reps rows 1 and 2 twice.

Row 7: p10, C5B, p8.

Row 8: k8, p5, k10.

Row 9: p8, T5R, k2, p8.

Row 10: k8, p2, k2, p3, k8.

Row 11: p6, T5R, p2, k2, p8.

Row 12: k8, p2, k4, p3, k6.

Row 13: p4, T5R, p4, k2, p8.

Row 14: k8, p2, k6, p3, k4.

Row 15: p4, T5L, p4, k2, p8.

Row 16: rep row 12.

Row 17: p6, T5L, p2, k2, p8.

Row 18: rep row 10.

Row 19: p8, T5L, k2, p8.

Row 20: rep row 8.

Row 21: p10, C5F, p8.

Row 22: rep row 8.

Row 23: p10, k5, p8.

Rows 24 and 25: rep rows 22 and 23.

Rows 26–34: rep rows 20–25, then rows 20–22 once more.

Row 35: p8, C4B, k1, C4F, p6.

Row 36: k6, p9, k8.

Row 37: p7, C3B, k5, C3F, p5.

Row 38: k5, p11, k7.

Row 39: p6, T3B, p1, k5, p1, T3F, p4.

Row 40: k4, p2, k2, p5, k2, p2, k6.

Row 41: p5, T3B, p2, k5, p2, T3F, p3.

Row 42: k3, p2, k4, p3, k4, p2, k5.

Row 43: p4, T3B, p5, k1, p5, T3F, p2.

Row 44: k2, p2, k13, p2, k4.

Row 45: p4, T3F, p11, T3B, p2.

Row 46: k3, p2, k11, p2, k5.

Row 47: p5, T3F, p9, T3B, p3.

Row 48: k4, p2, k9, p2, k6.

Row 49: p6, T4F, p5, T4B, p4.

Row 50: k6, p2, k5, p2, k8.

Row 51: p8, T4F, p1, T4B, p6.

Row 52: k8, p2, k1, p2, k10.

Row 53: rep row 21.

Row 54: rep row 8.

Rep rows 1–54 for patt.

BAG

Using 3.5 mm needles, cast on 92 sts (this is bottom of bag).

Work 1 row in seed st.

RS row: (work 23 st patt rep row 1 of chart) 4 times.

WS row: (work 23 st patt rep row 2 of chart) 4 times.

Rep these 2 rows twice more. Cable panels are now set.

Cont working rows 3–54, followed by rows 1–54 twice more as set.

Then cont working rows 1 and 2 of chart until piece measures 25 in [63.5 cm] from beg.

Knit 8 rows to form garter band.

Eyelet row: k7, *yfon, k2tog, k5, rep from * to last st, k1.

Purl 1 row, knit 8 rows. BO all sts.

BASE

Using 3.5 mm needles, cast on 14 sts, purl 1 row.

work first triangle as follows:

RS row: k13, wrap next st, turn, leave rem st unworked in hold.

WS: p13.

Next RS row: k12, wrap next st, turn, 2 sts now in hold. WS: p12.

Next RS row: k11, wrap next st, turn, 3 sts now in hold. WS: p11.

Cont in this way leaving an additional st in hold each RS row until the following 2 rows have been completed: RS row: k1, wrap next st, turn 13 sts now in hold and WS row: p1.

Knit across all sts picking up wraps.

work second triangle as follows:

WS row: p13, wrap next st, turn, leave rem st unworked in hold.

RS: k13.

Next WS row: p12, wrap next st, turn, 2 sts now in hold. RS: k12.

Next WS row: p11, wrap next st, turn, 3 sts now in hold. RS: k11.

Cont in this way leaving an additional st in hold each WS row until the following 2 rows have been completed: WS row: p1, wrap next st, turn, 13 sts now in hold and RS row: k1.

Purl across all sts picking up wraps.

Work third triangle as given for first triangle.

Work fourth triangle as given for second triangle.

Work fifth triangle as given for first triangle.

BO all sts. Sew bind-off edge to cast-on edge to form a circle.

STRAPS

Using pair of 3.5 mm dpns, make 3 4-stitch I-cords 26 in [66 cm] long and 1 4-stitch I-cord 40 in [101.5 cm] long.

FELTING

Place base and I-cords in a small laundry bag and place in washing machine with a few larger items (I suggest 2–3 pairs of jeans). Wash on hot with a cold rinse cycle using mild laundry soap. Block out pieces to dry. Base should now measure 5.5 in [14 cm] in diameter, if it is still larger than this, rep wash cycle until desired size is achieved.

FINISHING

Block bag piece to given dimensions. Join seam to make a tube. Sew base to bottom of bag.

Braid the 3 shorter I-cords together to make strap, secure ends together by sewing. Stitch strap in position, on seam where seam meets the base, and at the top just below the first garter band.

Thread longer I-cord through eyelets, beg and end at point opposite from seam. Knot ends to prevent slipping through holes during use.

make the inner base:
Cut a 5.5 in [14 cm] diameter circle from cardboard and place in the bottom of bag to reinforce.

Place yoga mat in bag, draw up cord to close opening, and tie. Take along to your next yoga class, trying not to allow your ego to be too proud.

mindfulness pointer: is knitting a hugging pose?

If you are making this bag, chances are that you are a yoga practitioner, so I don't need to overemphasize the point about being present and mindful as you knit. But notice that as you knit, your body and the work form a circle—that originates at your heart and passes down each arm and out through your hands—becoming a strong energy symbol. Aren't your arms in the same position as when hugging someone? So be mindful of the thoughts that occur to you as you knit; try to focus on loving kindness. In this way, the bag may become a capsule containing the energy those thoughts produced. It, too, completes a circle: It was made in homage to your love of yoga, and you applied yoga mindfulness as you were knitting.

sounds like fun

If we listened only to the information being broadcast by most media outlets, we would develop a very one-sided—and very bleak—view of our world. The never-ending barrage of disturbing, horrific images might lead us to believe that the world is made up only of destruction, suffering, and greed. What does being subjected to all this negative energy do to us?

There are times when I want to block out these less-than-beautiful aspects of our world and shift my focus from the images with which the media bombards us. This desire often leads me to seek the serenity of a garden or a park. We should all take a little quiet time now and then and visit a place where the volume of white noise from electronics is turned down, and the hum of bees, or children laughing, is turned up.

From my window, I can see into the playground of the local school. I love to sit in a chair by this window when I am writing or drinking coffee. Then one day as I was working at my computer, which is away from the window, I noticed that when I heard the bell ring for recess at the school, my mood lifted in response to the sound. I realized that I had come to associate the ringing bell with the joyful sound of children playing shortly afterward. Laughter is such a positive sound that it has the power to cut through the negativity emanating from my television and radio.

The cable in this project is placed in the center, flanked on each side by cords running parallel to it. The cords echo the central pattern in the same way that the echo of fun and laughter should ripple out into the world. The wave pattern at the lower edges is taken from the scientific, graphical depiction of sound energy, swinging from the negative to the all-important positive. The secret pocket is a place for a child to stash secret treasures, another source of fun.

SIZES / FINISHED CHEST
MEASUREMENTS

Small 26 in [66 cm]

Medium 28 in [71 cm]

Large 30 in [76 cm]

XL 32 in [81 cm]

Instructions are given for smallest size. If changes are necessary for larger sizes, the instructions are given in ( ). Where there is only one set of figures, this applies to all sizes.

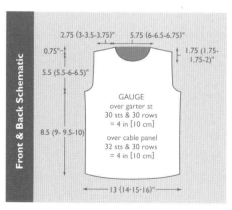

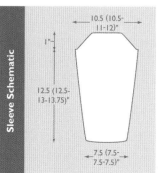

MATERIALS

DK Anti-tickle Merino Blend Superwash Wool by King Cole

M/C: shade 26 Bluebell, 8 (8-9-10) 50 g balls.

Color A: shade 47 Mauve, 1 50 g ball.

Color B: shade 118 Wild Rose, 1 50 g ball.

Color C: shade 18 Turquoise, 1 50 g ball.

Color D: shade 10 Amber, 1 50 g ball.

Pair of 4 mm needles, 3 stitch holders, cable needle.

Yarn amounts given are based on average requirements and are approximate.

TENSION / GAUGE

26 sts and 30 rows = 4 in [10 cm] over Fair Isle pattern.

13 rows of Chart A measures 1.75 in [4.5 cm].

32 sts and 30 rows over cable panel.

30 sts and 30 rows over garter stitch.

Take the time to check your gauge; change needle sizes if necessary to obtain correct gauge and garment size.

REFER TO GLOSSARY ON PAGE 13 FOR: GARTER STITCH, AND TO TECHNIQUES ON PAGE 12 FOR: FAIR ISLE TECHNIQUE.

Symbols Used in These Charts

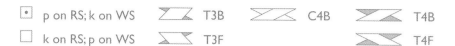

- ⊡ p on RS; k on WS
- ☐ k on RS; p on WS
- T3B
- T3F
- C4B
- T4B
- T4F

Chart A

Chart reads R to L RS rows and L to R WS rows

Chart Color Key
- ☐ C
- ☐ D

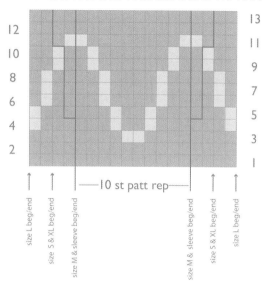

13
12
11
10
9
8
7
6
5
4
3
2
1

←10 st patt rep→

size L beg/end
size S & XL beg/end
size M & sleeve beg/end
size M & sleeve beg/end
size S & XL beg/end
size L beg/end

Chart B

Chart reads R to L RS rows and L to R WS rows

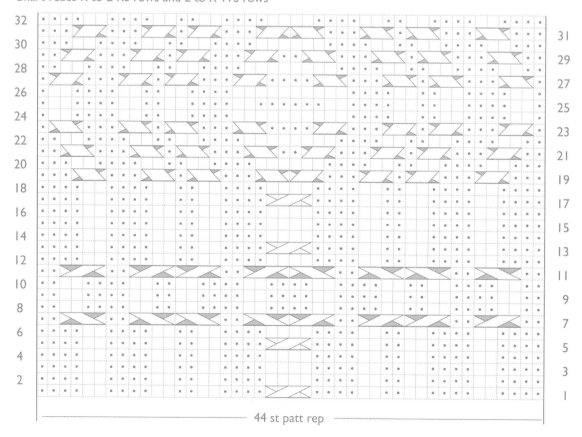

←—————————— 44 st patt rep ——————————→

PATTERN B

Row 1 (RS): (p4, k2) twice, p2, k2, p4, C4B, p4, k2, p2, (k2, p4) twice.

Row 2: (k4, p2) twice, k2, p2, k4, p4, k4, p2, k2, (p2, k4) twice.

Row 3: (p4, k2) twice, p2, k2, p4, k4, p4, k2, p2, (k2, p4) twice.

Rows 4–6: rep row 2, then rows 1 and 2 once more.

Row 7: (p2, T4B) twice, T4B, p2, T4B, T4F, p2, T4F, (T4F, p2) twice.

Row 8: k2, p2, k4, p2, k2, (p2, k4) 3 times, p2, k2, p2, k4, p2, k2.

Row 9: p2, k2, p4, k2, p2, k2, (p4, k2) 3 times, p2, k2, p4, k2, p2.

Row 10: rep row 8.

Row 11: (p2, T4F) twice, T4F, p2, T4F, T4B, p2, T4B, (T4B, p2) twice.

Row 12: rep row 2.

Rows 13–18: rep rows 1–6.

Row 19: (p3, T3B) twice, p1, T3B, p3, T3B, T3F, p3, T3F, p1, (T3F, p3) twice.

Row 20: k3, p2, k4, p2, k2, p2, k4, p6, k4, p2, k2, p2, k4, p2, k3.

Row 21: p2, T3B, p3, T3B, p1, T3B, p3, T3B, p2, T3F, p3, T3F, p1, T3F, p3, T3F, p2.

Row 22: k2, p2, k4, p2, k2, p2, k4, p8, k4, p2, k2, p2, k4, p2, k2.

Row 23: (p1, T3B, p3, T3B) twice, p4, (T3F, p3, T3F, p1) twice.

Row 24: k1, p2, k4, p2, k2, p2, k4, p10, k4, p2, k2, p2, k4, p2, k1.

Row 25: p1, k2, p4, k2, p2, k2, p4, k2, p6, k2, p4, k2, p2, k2, p4, k2, p1.

Row 26: rep row 24.

Row 27: (p1, T3F, p3, T3F) twice, p4, (T3B, p3, T3B, p1) twice.

Row 28: rep row 22.

Row 29: p2, T3F, p3, T3F, p1, T3F, p3, T3F, p2, T3B, p3, T3B, p1, T3B, p3, T3B, p2.

Row 30: rep row 20.

Row 31: (p3, T3F) twice, p1, T3F, p3, T3F, T3B, p3, T3B, p1, (T3B, p3) twice.

Row 32: rep row 2.

Rep rows 1–32 for patt B.

BACK

Using 4 mm needles and Color A, cast on 84 (90-98-104) sts. Knit 2 rows.

Change to Color B and knit 2 rows (forms garter ridges).

Working in St St and Fair Isle technique, place pattern as follows:

RS row: beg at RHS of chart as indicated for size, work 2 (0-4-2) edge sts, then work 10 st patt rep row 1 Chart A 8 (9-9-10) times, work 2 (0-4-2) edge sts.

WS row: beg at LHS of chart as indicated for size, work 2 (0-4-2) edge sts, then work 10 st patt rep row 2 Chart A 8 (9-9-10) times, work 2 (0-4-2) edge sts.

Work rows 3–13 Chart A in sequence as now set.

Change to Color B, purl 2 rows.

Change to Color A, purl 2 rows (garter ridges).

Change to M/C, purl next row working incs as follows:

Inc row: p30 (33-37-40), (inc in next st by working into it twice, p7) 3 times, inc in next st, purl to end, 88 (94-102-108) sts.

Working in M/C throughout, work set-up rows as follows:

RS row: k22 (25-29-32), (p4, k2) twice, p2, k2, p4, k4, p4, k2, p2, (k2, p4) twice, k22 (25-29-32).

WS row: k22 (25-29-32), (k4, p2) twice, k2, p2, k4, p4, k4, p2, k2, (p2, k4) twice, k22 (25-29-32).

***Place center panel as follows, place markers to designate center panel as indicated:

RS row: k22 (25-29-32), place marker, work row 1 Chart B, place marker, k22 (25-29-32).

WS row: k22 (25-29-32), work row 2 Chart B, k22 (25-29-32).

Cont working chart rows in sequence as set, until piece measures 8.5 (9-9.5-10) in [21.5 (23-24-25) cm], end RS row facing for next row.

shape armholes as follows:
Cont in patt as set, BO 4 sts at beg of next 2 rows, and 3 sts at beg of following 2 rows, 74 (80-88-94) sts rem.

Work even until piece measures 5.5 (5.5-6-6.5) in [14 (14-15-16.5) cm] from beg of armhole shaping, end with RS row facing for next row.

shape shoulders as follows:

BO 6 (7-8-8) sts at beg of next 4 rows, and 6 (6-7-9) sts at beg of following 2 rows. Leave rem 38 (40-42-44) sts on a stitch holder.

FRONT

make secret pocket lining as follows:

Using 4 mm needles and M/C, cast on 18 (20-22-24) sts. Beg with a knit row work 20 rows in St St. Leave sts on a spare needle.

Work as given for back until inc row has been worked.

attach pocket on RS set-up row as follows:

Using M/C, k4 (5-7-8), knit next st on LH needle tog with 1st st from pocket lining, rep with next st from LH needle and 2nd st from lining, slip next 14 (16-18-20) sts from LH needle onto a stitch holder, knit across next 14 (16-18-20) sts from pocket lining, knit next st on LH needle tog with 2nd last st from pocket lining, rep with next st from LH needle and last st from lining, (p4, k2) twice, p2, k2, p4, k4, p4, k2, p2, (k2, p4) twice, k22 (25-29-32).

Work WS set-up row as given for back.

Now follow instructions as given for Back from *** until armhole shaping has been completed.

Work in patt without further dec until piece measures 3.75 (3.75-4.25-4.5) in [9.5 (9.5-11-11.5) cm] from beg of armhole shaping, end RS row facing for next row.

shape front neck and shoulders as follows:

Cont in patt as set, work across 28 (30-33-35) sts, turn (this is neck edge). Leave rem 46 (50-55-59) sts on a spare needle. Working on the 28 (30-33-35) sts only, cont in patt dec 1 st at neck edge on following 10 rows, 18 (20-23-25) sts rem. Work 3 (3-3-5) rows even, end RS row facing for next row.

Bind off 6 (7-8-8) sts at beg of row. Work WS row even.

Rep the last 2 rows once more. Then BO rem 6 (6-7-9) sts.

Return to sts on spare needle. Slip center 18 (20-22-24) st onto a stitch holder. Rejoin yarn to rem sts and work to end. Dec 1 st at neck edge on next 10 rows, 18 (20-23-25) sts rem. Work 4 (4-4-6) rows even, end WS row facing for next row.

BO 6 (7-8-8) sts at beg of row. Work RS row even.

Rep the last 2 rows once more. BO rem 6 (6-7-9) sts.

SLEEVE (MAKE 2 ALIKE)

Using 4 mm needles and Color A, cast on 50 sts. Knit 2 rows.

Change to Color B, knit 2 rows, (garter ridges).

Working in St St and Fair Isle technique, place pattern as follows:

RS row: work 10 st patt rep row 1 Chart A 5 times.

WS row: work 10 st patt rep row 2 Chart A 5 times.

Work rows 3–13 in sequence as now set, *at the same time* inc 1 st at each end of rows 5 and 11 work inc sts in patt, 54 sts.

Change to Color B, purl 2 rows.

Change to Color A, purl 2 rows.

Change to M/C, purl next row working incs as follows:

Inc in first st, p14 (14-15-16), (inc in next st, p7) 3 times, inc in next st, purl to last st, inc in last st, 60 sts.

Working in M/C throughout, work set-up rows as follows:

RS row: k8, (p4, k2) twice, p2, k2, p4, k4, p4, k2, p2, (k2, p4) twice, k8.

WS row: k8, (k4, p2) twice, k2, p2, k4, p4, k4, p2, k2, (p2, k4) twice, k8.

Now place cable panel as follows, place markers to designate its position:

RS row: k8, place marker, work row 1 Chart B, place marker, k8.

WS row: k8, work row 2 Chart B, k8.

Cont working chart rows in sequence as set, *at the same time* inc 1 st at each end of row 3 and every following 8th row 8 (8-0-1) times, 78 (78-62-64) sts, work all inc sts into garter st (knit every row) throughout. Then inc 1 st at each end of every following 6th row 0 (0-11-13) times, 78 (78-84-90) sts. Work without further inc until sleeve measures 12.5 (12.5-13-13.75) in [31.75 (31.75-33-35) cm] from beg.

shape cap as follows:

BO 4 (4-4-5) sts at beg of next 2 rows and 3 (3-4-5) sts at beg of following 4 rows. BO rem 58 (58-60-60) sts.

FINISHING AND NECKBAND

Weave in ends. Block all pieces to given dimensions. Join RHS shoulder seam.

With RS facing and beg at LH shoulder, using 4 mm needles and Color B pick up and knit 12 (13-14-16) sts down LHS front neck, knit across 18 (20-22-24) sts from front neck st holder, pick up and knit 12 (13-14-16) up RHS front neck, knit across 38 (40-42-44) sts from back neck st holder, 80 (86-92-100) sts total.

Knit 1 row. Change to Color A, knit 2 rows. BO all sts.

Set in sleeves to armholes. Sew side and sleeve seams. Using M/C and 4 mm needles, place pocket-lining sts onto needle and BO.

Slip st pocket lining to WS of front.

Press lightly, following the instructions on the yarn label.

mindfulness pointer: have fun with numbers

Just as I had hoped, my test knitter, Carole, had fun working on this project, especially the secret pocket. She told me how she enjoyed the rhythm of the cable panel, and how she found it soothing to count the stitches. It reminded me of songs from my school days: "Two, four, six, eight, who do we appreciate," "One, two, buckle my shoe," "Three, six, nine, the goose drank wine." As you knit, take a stroll down memory lane to remind yourself of your favorite number songs. I promise it will bring a smile to your face. There is power in the energy created by sound, so why not add to the fun in the world by teaching these songs to little ones?

beachcombing

Sometimes, simple pleasures can serve to bring our lives into clear perspective. For me, walking barefoot along a beach is one of those simple pleasures. It connects me to my body through tactile pleasures: the feel of wet sand between my toes, the lap of cool water around my ankles, the sharp stab of a broken seashell, the warmth of the sun on my face, or the wind in my hair. At the same time, it reminds me of the greater whole, of the powerful forces of nature: flotsam washed up on the shore from far away, carried by the tides that are controlled by the moon, the smoothness of pebbles eroded by water over eons of time. I think of the energetic rhythms of the world, the monthly phases of the moon, the yearly changes of the seasons, the decades of erosion and accumulation— of things begun before I was born that will continue long after I am gone.

I love to ponder these ideas, to remind myself that my petty concerns are insignificant in the scheme of things. A few hours at the beach can restore my energy like nothing else.

The rhythmic movement of the cables in this pillow draws its inspiration from the ripple patterns left in wet sand by a retreating tide. I cannot always be at the shore, so this project brings a little memory of it to my home.

FINISHED MEASUREMENTS

16 x 16 in [40.5 x 40.5 cm] when finished

MATERIALS

Eco Knit Cotton, 50 g skeins in the following quantities and shades:

2 skeins, 01 Cream

3 skeins, 02 Cinnamon

4 skeins, 03 Sage

2 skeins, 04 Olive

2 skeins, 05 Coffee

Pair of 4 mm needles, CN, 16 x 16 in [40.5 x 40.5 cm] pillow form, 5 buttons (look in your box or make your own).

Yarn amounts given are based on average requirements and are approximate.

TENSION / GAUGE

28 sts and 30 rows = 4 in [10 cm] over cable pattern.

Take the time to check your gauge; change needle sizes if necessary to obtain correct gauge and garment size.

REFER TO GLOSSARY ON PAGE 13 FOR: GARTER STITCH.

STRIPE SEQUENCE

**=change color as indicated:
Rows 1–6 Cream
Rows 7–14 Cinnamon
Rows 15–18 Coffee
Rows 19–22 Olive
Rows 23–32 Sage

•	p on RS; k on WS	T4R		T5R	
	k on RS; p on WS	T4L		T5L	

Chart reads R to L RS rows and L to R WS rows

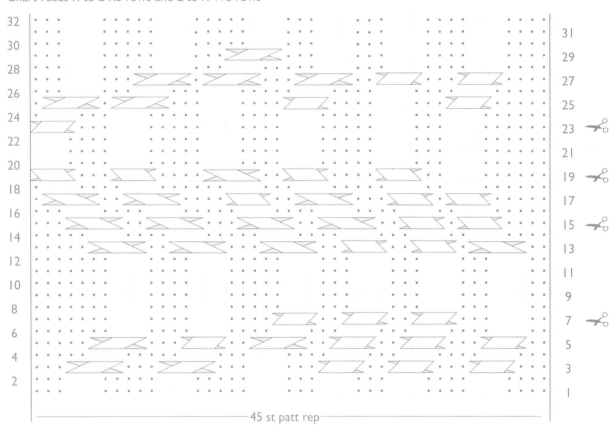

—⊱ Change color as indicated by stripe sequence

Please see note on placing markers in Things You Need to Know Before You Begin (p.8)

CABLE PATTERN

Row 1 (RS): (p4, k3) twice, (p3, k3) twice, (p5, k3) twice, p3.

Row 2: k3, (p3, k5) twice, (p3, k3) twice, (p3, k4) twice.

Row 3: (p3, T4R) twice, p2, T4R, p3, k3, (p3, T5R) twice, p3.

Row 4: (k5, p3) twice, (k3, p3, k4, p3) twice, k3.

Row 5: p2, T4R, p3, (T4R, p2) twice, T5R, p2, T4R, p3, T5R, p5.

Row 6: k7, (p3, k4) twice, (p3, k3) twice, p3, k4, p3, k2.

**Row 7: p2, k3, p3, (T4R, p2) twice, T4R, (p4, k3) twice, p7.

Row 8: k7, p3, k4, p3, k5, (p3, k3) 3 times, p3, k2.

Row 9: p2, (k3, p3) 3 times, k3, p5, k3, p4, k3, p7.

Row 10: rep row 8.

Row 11: rep row 9.

Row 12: rep row 8.

Row 13: p2, T5L, p1, (T4L, p2) twice, T5L, p3, T5L, p2,

T5L, p5.

Row 14: (k5, p3, k4, p3) twice, k3, p3, k2, p3, k4.

**Row 15: p4, T4L, p1, T4L, (p2, T5L) twice, p3, T5L, p2, T5L, p3.

Row 16: k3, p3, k4, p3, k5, p3, k4, p3, k4, p3, k2, p3, k5.

Row 17: p5, T4L, p1, T4L, p3, T5L, p2, T4L, p4, T5L, p2, T5L, p1.

Row 18: k1, p3, k4, p3, k6, p3, k3, p3, k5, p3, k2, p3, k6.

**Row 19: p6, k3, p2, T4L,

p4, T4L, p2, T5L, p4, T4L, p3, T4L.

Row 20: (p3, k4, p3, k5) twice, p3, k3, p3, k6.

Row 21: p6, k3, p3, k3, (p5, k3, p4, k3) twice.

Row 22: rep row 20.

**Row 23: p6, k3, p3, k3, p5, k3, p4, k3, p5, k3, p3, T4R.

Row 24: k1, p3, k3, p3, k5, p3, k4, p3, k5, p3, k3, p3, k6.

Row 25: p5, T4R, p3, k3, p4, T4R, p4, k3, p3, (T5R, p1) twice.

Row 26: (k3, p3) 3 times, k5, (p3, k4) twice, p3, k5.

Row 27: p4, T4R, p3, T4R, p2, T5R, p3, T5R, p1, T5R, p3, k3, p3.

Row 28: (k3, p3, k5, p3) twice, k3, p3, k4, p3, k4.

Row 29: (p4, k3) twice, p3, k3, p3, T5R, p3, k3, p5, k3, p3.

Row 30: rep row 2.

Row 31: rep row 1.

Row 32: rep row 2.

Rep rows 1–32 for patt.

FIRST KNITTED PIECE

Using Cream and 4 mm needles, cast on 186 sts, knit 1 row. Place patt as follows:

Row 1 (RS): p3, (work 45 st patt rep row 1 of chart) 4 times, p3.

Row 2: k3, (work 45 st patt rep row 2 of chart) 4 times, k3.

Cont working chart rows in sequence as set, changing colors as indicated until rows 1–32 have been worked 3 times, piece will measure approx 12.5 in [32 cm] from beg. BO all sts, place marker in corner at end of BO row.

SECOND KNITTED PIECE

With RS facing, using Cream and 4 mm needles, pick up and knit 96 sts along side edge (opposite from marker) of first piece.

WS row: k3, (work 45 st patt rep given row 2 of chart) twice, k3.

Row 1 (RS): p3, (work 45 st patt rep given for row 1 of chart) twice, p3.

Row 2: k3, work 45 st patt rep given row 2 of chart twice, k3.

Cont working chart rows in sequence as set changing colors as indicated until rows 1–32 have been worked twice, piece will measure approx 8.5 in [21.5 cm] from pick-up row. BO all sts. Place 2nd marker in corner at end of BO row.

Sew second piece to first piece to form a tube, matching markers together (this is the top edge). Remove markers. Fold pillow in half, placing pick-up and bind off edges of second piece together, both first and second pieces will be folded in half.

With RS facing, using Sage and 4 mm needle, beg at fold in second piece, working along top edge, to fold in first piece, pick up and knit 90 sts. Knit 8 rows to form garter stitch band. BO all sts.

With RS facing, using Sage and 4 mm needle, beg at fold in first piece, working along top edge to fold in second piece, pick up and knit 90 sts. Knit 56 rows to form garter stitch band. BO all sts.

FINISHING AND JOINING UP

Weave in all ends. Block piece to given dimensions. Sew lower edge seam.

Fold longer garter band over shorter one to overlap. Stitch side seams at garter bands in this position. Place pillow form into cover. Stitch buttons in position spaced evenly as shown on photograph, stitch through both garter bands to close.

mindfulness pointer: learn from simple pleasures

Let the knitting flow and be mindful of the patterns you are creating, like those raked in the sand of a Zen garden. If you find that you have deviated from my pattern, try following it to see where it takes you. Don't rip out your knitting unless it looks awkward or angular—you are aiming for soft undulations. You may choose to vary the pattern slightly in each piece, and experience the energy released by the thrill of figuring something out for yourself. Try making the buttons by using found objects such as shells, pebbles, driftwood, or other items from your box of treasures.

potential energy

Sometimes a design evolves from a series of ideas and in reaction to a variety of impulses. Each impulse has the potential to spark a design and contains its own energy. The design for this sweater evolved from a series of seemingly unrelated ideas, including charkas, acupuncture meridians and the concept of the conversion of energy from one state to another. As I explored each, the image of a coiled spring emerged becoming the basis for these cables. Ancient schools of wisdom depict the body's stored energy as coiled. We also liken a cat ready to pounce, or a sprinter preparing for a race to a coiled spring, as they anticipate the moment of take-off. The parallel lines used here trace those commonly used to depict energy meridians within the body. It is also not surprising that they accentuate the power of a man's upper body.

SIZES / FINISHED CHEST
MEASUREMENTS
Small 44 in [112 cm]
Medium 48 in [122 cm]
Large 52 in [132 cm]
XL 56 in [142 cm]

Instructions are given for smallest size. If changes are necessary for larger sizes, the instructions are given in ( ). Where there is only one set of figures, this applies to all sizes.

MATERIALS

M/C: 100% Silk by Estelle Designs, shade 139, 12 (13-14-15) 50 g balls.

Color A: 100% Silk by Estelle Designs, shade 140, 1 50 g ball.

Pair of 4 mm needles, circular (26 in [66 cm] long) 4 mm needle (used for neckline), CN, 1 stitch holder.

Yarn amounts given are based on average requirements and are approximate.

TENSION / GAUGE
20 sts and 28 rows = 4 in [10 cm] over cable pattern.

16 sts and 28 rows = 4 in [10 cm] over stockinette stitch.

Take the time to check your gauge; change needle sizes if necessary to obtain correct gauge and garment size.

REFER TO GLOSSARY ON PAGE 13 FOR: SEED STITCH.

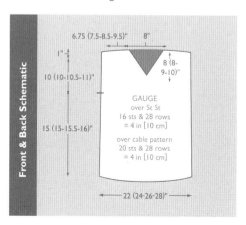

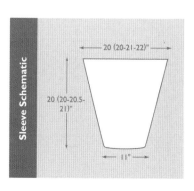

Symbols Used in The Following Charts

⊡ p on RS; k on WS   ☐ k on RS; p on WS

▱ C3B   ▱ C3F   ▱ T3B

▱ T3F

Chart A

Chart reads R to L RS rows and L to R WS rows

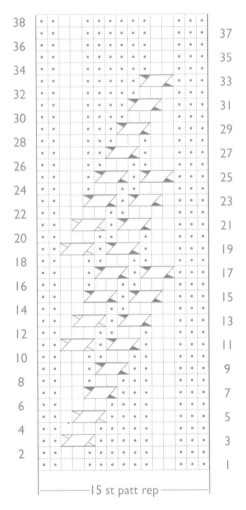

—15 st patt rep—

PATTERN A

Row 1 (RS): p3, k2, p6, k2, p2.

Row 2: k2, p2, k6, p2, k3.

Row 3: p3, k2, p5, C3B, p2.

Row 4: k2, p3, k5, p2, k3.

Row 5: p3, k2, p4, C3B, k1, p2.

Row 6: k2, p4, k4, p2, k3.

Chart B

Chart reads R to L RS rows and L to R WS rows

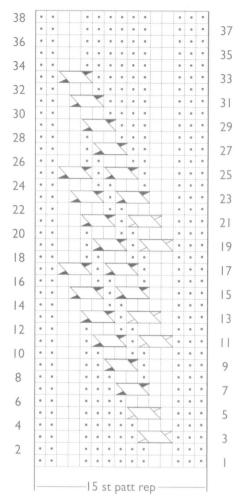

—I5 st patt rep—

Please see note on placing markers in Things You Need to Know Before You Begin (p.8)

Row 7: p3, k2, p3, T3B, k2, p2.

Row 8: k2, p2, kI, p2, k3, p2, k3.

Row 9: p3, k2, p2, T3B, pI, k2, p2.

Row 10: (k2, p2) 3 times, k3.

Row 11: p3, k2, pI, T3B, pI, C3B, p2.

Row 12: k2, p3, k2, p2, kI, p2, k3.

Row 13: p3, k2, T3B, pI, C3B, kI, p2.

Row 14: (k2, p4) twice, k3.

Row 15: p3, kI, T3B, pI, T3B, k2, p2.

Row 16: k2, p2, kI, p2, k2, p3, k3.

Row 17: p3, (T3B, pI) twice, k2, p2.

Row 18: rep row 10.

Row 19: p3, k2, pI, T3B, pI, C3B, p2.

Row 20: k2, p3, k2, p2, kI, p2, k3.

Row 21: p3, k2, T3B, pI, C3B, kI, p2.

Rows 22–25: rep rows 14–17.

Row 26: rep row 10.

Row 27: p3, k2, pI, T3B, p2, k2, p2.

Row 28: k2, p2, k3, p2, kI, p2, k3.

Row 29: p3, k2, T3B, p3, k2, p2.

Row 30: k2, p2, k4, p4, k3.

Row 31: p3, kI, T3B, p4, k2, p2.

Row 32: k2, p2, k5, p3, k3.

Row 33: p3, T3B, p5, k2, p2.

Row 34: rep row 2.

Rows 35–38: rep rows I and 2 twice.

Rep rows I–38 for patt A.

PATTERN B

Row I (RS): p3, k2, p6, k2, p2.

Row 2: k2, p2, k6, p2, k3.

Row 3: p3, C3F, p5, k2, p2.

Row 4: k2, p2, k5, p3, k3.

Row 5: p3, kI, C3F, p4, k2, p2.

Row 6: k2, p2, k4, p4, k3.

Row 7: p3, k2, T3F, p3, k2, p2.

Row 8: k2, p2, k3, p2, kI, p2, k3.

Row 9: p3, k2, pI, T3F, p2, k2, p2.

Row 10: (k2, p2) 3 times, k3.

Row 11: p3, C3F, pI, T3F, pI, k2, p2.

Row 12: k2, p2, kI, p2, k2, p3, k3.

Row 13: p3, kI, C3F, pI, T3F, k2, p2.

Row 14: (k2, p4) twice, k3.

Row 15: p3, k2, T3F, pI, T3F, kI, p2.

Row 16: k2, p3, k2, p2, kI, p2, k3.

Row 17: p3, k2, (pI, T3F) twice, p2.

Row 18: rep row 10.

Row 19: p3, C3F, pI, T3F, pI, k2, p2.

Row 20: k2, p2, kI, p2, k2, p3, k3.

Row 21: p3, kI, C3F, pI, T3F, k2, p2.

Rows 22–25: rep rows 14–17.

Row 26: rep row 10.

Row 27: p3, k2, p2, T3F, pI, k2, p2.

Row 28: k2, p2, kI, p2, k3, p2, k3.

Row 29: p3, k2, p3,T3F, k2, p2.

Row 30: k2, p4, k4, p2, k3.

Row 31: p3, k2, p4, T3F, kI, p2.

Row 32: k2, p3, k5, p2, k3.

Row 33: p3, k2, p5, T3F, p2.

Row 34: rep row 2.

Rows 35–38: rep rows I and 2 twice.

Rep rows I–38 for patt B.

Symbols Used in This Chart

⊡ p on RS; k on WS ☐ k on RS; p on WS ▱ T3B ▱ T3F

Chart C

Chart reads R to L RS rows and L to R WS rows

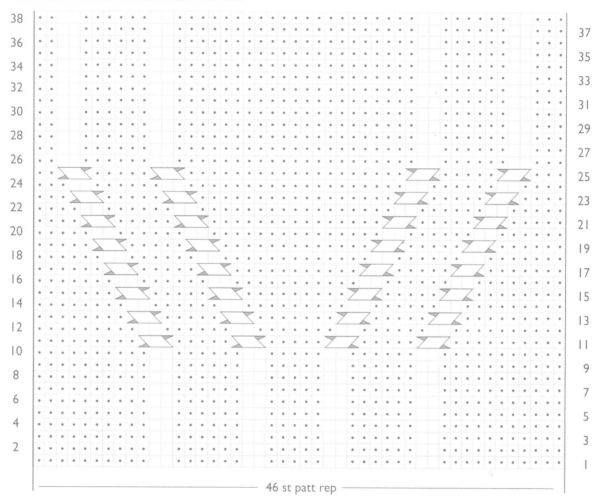

46 st patt rep

Please see note on placing markers in Things You Need to Know Before You Begin (p.8)

PATTERN C

Row 1 (RS): p11, k2, p6, k2, p5, k2, p6, k2, p10.

Row 2: k10, p2, k6, p2, k5, p2, k6, p2, k11.

Rows 3–10: rep rows 1 and 2, 4 times.

Row 11: p10, (T3B, p5) twice, T3F, p5, T3F, p9.

Row 12: k9, p2, k6, p2, k7, p2, k6, p2, k10.

Row 13: p9, T3B, p5, T3B, p7, T3F, p5, T3F, p8.

Row 14: k8, p2, k6, p2, k9, p2, k6, p2, k9.

Row 15: p8, T3B, p5, T3B, p9, T3F, p5, T3F, p7.

Row 16: k7, p2, k6, p2, k11, p2, k6, p2, k8.

Row 17: p7, T3B, p5, T3B, p11, T3F, p5, T3F, p6.

Row 18: (k6, p2) twice, k13, p2, k6, p2, k7.

Row 19: p6, T3B, p5, T3B, p13, (T3F, p5) twice.

Row 20: k5, p2, k6, p2, k15, (p2, k6) twice.

Row 21: (p5, T3B) twice, p15, T3F, p5, T3F, p4.

Row 22: k4, p2, k6, p2, k17, p2, k6, p2, k5

Row 23: p4, T3B, p5, T3B, p17, T3F, p5, T3F, p3.

Row 24: k3, p2, k6, p2, k19, p2, k6, p2, k4.

Row 25: p3, T3B, p5, T3B, p19, T3F, p5, T3F, p2.

Row 26: k2, p2, k6, p2, k21, p2, k6, p2, k3.

Row 27: p3, k2, p6, k2, p21, k2, p6, k2, p2.

Row 28: rep row 26.

Rows 29–38: rep rows 27 and 28, 5 times.

BACK

Using Color A cast on 104 (112-120-128) sts and work 6 rows in seed st.

Change to M/C and place pattern as follows:

Note: place markers to designate each chart position.

Row 1 (RS): p14 (18-22-26), work row 1 Chart A, p8, work row 1 Chart A again, work row 1 Chart B, p8, work row 1 Chart B again, p14 (18-22-26).

Row 2: k14 (18-22-26), work row 2 Chart B, k8, work row 2 Chart B again, work row 2 Chart A, k8, work row 2 Chart A again, k14 (18-22-26).

Cont working chart rows in sequence as set until 2 patt reps are completed (rows 1–38 twice),

piece measures approximately 12 in [30 cm] from beg.

work transition as follows:
Note: change placement of markers to designate center panel as indicated below.

Row 1 (RS): p14 (18-22-26), work row 1 Chart A, place marker, work as given row 1 Chart C, place second marker, work row 1 Chart B, p14 (18-22-26).

Row 2: k14 (18-22-26), work row 2 Chart B, work as given row 2 Chart C, work row 2 Chart A, k14 (18-22-26).

Work charts rows 3–38 in sequence as set.

establish new pattern placement as follows:

Row 1 (RS): p14 (18-22-26), (work row 1 Chart A) twice, p16, (work row 1 Chart B) twice, p14 (18-22-26).

Row 2: k14 (18-22-26), (work row 2 Chart B) twice, k16, (work row 2 Chart A) twice, k14 (18-22-26).

Cont working chart rows in sequence as <u>now</u> set until piece measures 25 (25-26-27) in [63.5 (63.5-66-68.5) cm] from beg, end with RS row facing for next row.

shape shoulders as follows:
Working in patt as set BO 11 (12-13-15) sts at beg of next 4 rows. Then BO 10 (12-14-14) sts at beg of following 2 rows. Leave rem 40 sts on a stitch holder.

FRONT

Work as given for back until row 28 of transition (Chart C) has been completed. Piece will now measure approx 16 in [40 cm].

Working in patt as set (rows 29–38 Chart C),

shape V neck as follows:
RS row: work across 49 (53-57-61) sts in patt, p2togb, p1, turn. Leave rem 52 (56-60-64) sts on a spare needle for RHS.

Working on the sts from LHS only:

WS row: k2, work in patt to end.

RS row: work to last 3 sts in patt, p2togb, p1.

Rep last WS row.

Rep the last 2 rows 3 more times, row 38 Chart C completed, 47 (51-55-59) sts rem.

establish new pattern placement as follows:
Row 1 (RS): p14 (18-22-26), (work row 1 Chart A) twice, p2togb, p1.

Row 2: k2, (work row 2 Chart A) twice, k14 (18-22-26).

Cont working chart rows in sequence as <u>now</u> set, dec 1 st at neck (as before) on every RS row 14 more times 32 (36-40-44) sts rem, work all WS rows even.

Work even in patt until piece measures same as back before shoulder shaping, end RS row facing for next row.

shape shoulder as follows:

RS row: BO 11 (12-13-15) sts at beg of row, work in patt to last 2 sts, p2.

WS row: k2, work in patt to end.

Rep the last 2 rows once more. BO rem 10 (12-14-14) sts.

Return to the 52 (56-60-64) sts on the spare needle, rejoin yarn and working in patt as set following rows 29–38 Chart C as follows:

RS row: p1, p2tog, work in patt to end.

WS row: work in patt to last 2 sts, k2.

Rep the last 2 rows 4 more times, row 38 of Chart C completed, 47 (51-55-59) sts rem.

establish new pattern placement as follows:

Row 1 (RS): p1, p2tog, (work row 1 Chart B) twice, p14 (18-22-26).

Row 2: k14 (18-22-26), (work row 2 Chart B) twice, k2.

Cont working chart rows in sequence as <u>now</u> set, dec 1 st at neck (as before) on every RS row 14 more times 32 (34-40-44) sts rem, work all WS rows even.

Work even in patt until piece measures same as back before shoulder shaping, end WS row facing for next row.

shape shoulder as follows:

WS row: BO 11 (12-13-15) sts at beg of row, work in patt to last 2 sts, k2.

RS row: p2, work in patt to end.

Rep the last 2 rows once more. BO rem 10 (12-14-14) sts.

SLEEVE (MAKE 2 ALIKE)

Using Color A cast on 54 sts and work 6 rows in seed st.

Change to M/C and place pattern as follows:

Row 1 (RS): p12, work row 1 Chart A, followed by row 1 Chart B, p12.

Row 2: k12, work row 2 Chart B, followed by row 2 Chart A, k12.

Cont working chart rows in sequence as set, *at the same time* inc 1 st at each end of row 3 (3-3-5) and every following 6th row 7 (7-16-21) times, 70 (70-88-98) sts. Work inc sts in rev St St throughout. Then inc 1 st at each end of

every following 8th row 10 (10-3-0) times, 90 (90-94-98) sts. Work even in patt until piece measures 20 (20-20.5-21) in [51 (51-52-53.5) cm] from beg. BO loosely.

FINISHING AND NECKBAND

Weave in ends. Block all pieces to given dimensions. Join both shoulder seams.

Using Color A and circular 4 mm needle, beg at CF with RS facing, pick up and knit 50 sts up RHS of V neck, knit across 40 sts from back neck stitch holder, then pick up and knit 50 sts down LHS of V neck, 140 sts. Working back and forth, work 6 rows in seed st. BO all sts in patt.

Cross LHS neckband over RHS neckband at CF and stitch both ends in place to pick up row.

Place marker on each side seam 10 (10-10.5-11) in [25-5 (25.5-26.5-28) cm] down from shoulder. Sew in sleeves between markers. Sew side and sleeve seams. Press lightly, following the instructions on the yarn label.

mindfulness pointer: energy stores

Have you ever noticed that yarn seems to come with its own supply of potential energy? In the spinning process, fibers are twisted together into yarn by means of electrical (or human) power. This power is converted to the tension stored within the strand of yarn. Your energy is then infused into a piece during the act of knitting. You will notice this if you have to rip out your knitting—the shapes of the stitches you formed still remain in the kinks of the yarn. You can see all this stored energy the moment you open your knitting basket and your knitting springs out, making a bid for freedom. So never underestimate the power of a hand-knitted sweater!

power cables unplugged

In August 2003, I was struck by two seemingly unrelated events that occurred exactly one week apart. The first was a power outage that left most of the eastern seaboard without electricity; the second was a huge summer storm. The striking photographs of these events on the front pages of the newspaper caught my attention.

The blackout garnered lots of attention, whereas the storm the following week might have remained unreported had it not been a slow news day. The newspaper ran a photograph of a very impressive streak of lightning illuminating the skyline of the city in the storm. This was in complete contrast to the blackout of the previous week, when a photograph of the city in total darkness made the paper. The thought crossed my mind that once again Mother Nature had shown her capabilities, whereas man's invention had failed spectacularly just seven days before.

Inspired by this thought, I set about designing a cable that would bring these two events together. The common denominator, of course, was electricity. The zigzag cable in this pattern represents a streak of lightning with its ends dissipating power in both directions, to the heavens above and to the earth below. Each repeat is broken and slightly offset from one another—interrupted to represent the failure of the grid on August 14.

SIZES / FINISHED CHEST MEASUREMENTS

Small 36 in [91.5 cm]
Medium 39 in [99 cm]
Large 42 in [106.5 cm]
XL 45 in [114 cm]
2X 48 in [122 cm]

Instructions are given for smallest size. If changes are necessary for larger sizes, the instructions are given in ( ). Where there is only one set of figures this applies to all sizes.

MATERIALS

Summer Tweed by Rowan shade 536, 11 (11-12-13-14) 50 g skeins.

Pair of 5 mm needles, CN, 2 stitch holders.

Yarn amounts given are based on average requirements and are approximate.

TENSION / GAUGE

20 sts and 26 rows = 4 in [10 cm] over cable pattern.

Take the time to check your gauge; change needle sizes if necessary to obtain correct gauge and garment size.

REFER TO GLOSSARY ON PAGE 13 FOR: SEED STITCH.

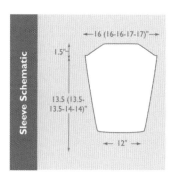

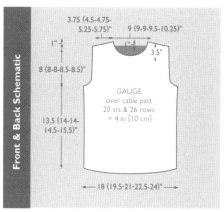

Symbols Used in These Charts

⊡	p on RS; k on WS
☐	k on RS; p on WS

C4B C4F T4B T4F T5R T5L C6B C6F T6B T6F

Chart A

Chart reads R to L RS rows and L to R WS rows

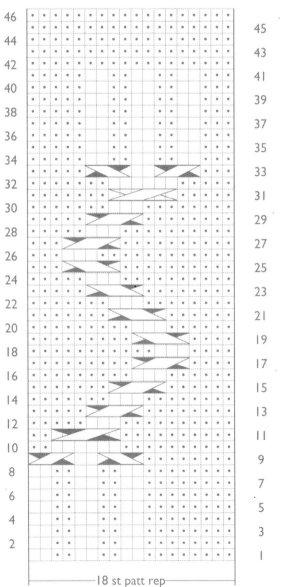

├─18 st patt rep─┤

Please see note on placing markers in
Things You Need to Know Before You Begin (p.8)

Chart B

Chart reads R to L RS rows and L to R WS rows

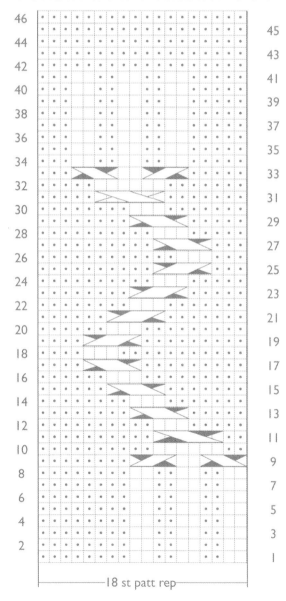

├─18 st patt rep─┤

Please see note on placing markers in
Things You Need to Know Before You Begin (p.8)

PATTERN A

Row 1 (RS): p8, (k2, p2) twice, k2.

Row 2: p2 (k2, p2) twice, k8.

Rows 3–8: rep rows 1 and 2, 3 times.

Row 9: p8, T4F, k2, T4B.

Row 10: k2, p6, k10.

Row 11: p10, T6B, p2.

Row 12: k5, p3, k10.

Row 13: p8, T5R, p5.

Row 14: k7, p3, k8.

Row 15: p6, T5R, p7.

Row 16: k9, p3, k6.

Row 17: p4 T5R, p9.

Row 18: k11, p3, k4.

Row 19: p4, T5L, p9.

Row 20: k9, p3, k6.

Row 21: p6, T5L, p7.

Row 22: rep row 14.

Row 23: p8, T5L, p5.

Row 24: rep row 12.

Row 25: p10, T5L, p3.

Row 26: k3, p3, k12.

Row 27: p10, T5R, p3.

Row 28: rep row 12.

Row 29: p8, T5R, p5.

Row 30: rep row 14.

Row 31: p5, C6B, p7.

Row 32: k7, p6, k5.

Row 33: p3, T4B, k2, T4F, p5.

Row 34: k5, (p2, k2) twice, p2, k3.

Row 35: p3, (k2, p2) twice, k2, p5.

Rows 36–41: rep rows 34 and 35, 3 times.

Row 42: knit all sts.

Row 43: purl all sts.

Rows 44–46: rep rows 42 and 43 once, then row 42 once more.

Rep rows 1–46 for patt A.

PATTERN B

Row 1 (RS): (k2, p2) twice, k2, p8.

Row 2: k8, (p2, k2) twice, p2.

Rows 3–8: rep rows 1 and 2, 3 more times.

Row 9: T4F, k2, T4B, p8.

Row 10: k10, p6, k2.

Row 11: p2, T6F, p10.

Row 12: k10, p3, k5.

Row 13: p5, T5L, p8.

Row 14: k8, p3, k7.

Row 15: p7, T5L, p6.

Row 16: k6, p3, k9.

Row 17: p9, T5L, p4.

Row 18: k4, p3, k11.

Row 19: p9, T5R, p4.

Row 20: k6, p3, k9.

Row 21: p7, T5R, p6.

Row 22: rep row 14.

Row 23: p5, T5R, p8.

Row 24: rep row 12.

Row 25: p3, T5R, k10.

Row 26: k12, p3, k3.

Row 27: p3, T5L, p10.

Row 28: rep row 12.

Row 29: p5, T5L, p8.

Row 30: rep row 14.

Row 31: p7, C6F, p5.

Row 32: k5, p6, k7.

Row 33: p5, T4B, k2, T4F, p3.

Row 34: k3, (p2, k2) twice, p2, k5.

Row 35: p5, (k2, p2) twice, k2, p3.

Rows 36–41: rep rows 34 and 35, 3 times.

Row 42: knit all sts.

Row 43: purl all sts.

Rows 44–46: rep rows 42 and 43 once, then row 42 once more.

Rep rows 1–46 for patt B.

BACK

Using 5 mm needles, cast on 90 (98-106-112-120) sts. Work 2 rows in seed st, then place pattern as follows:

RS: p9 (4-8-11-6), work 18 st patt rep row 1 Chart A 4 (5-5-5-6) times, p9 (4-8-11-6).

WS: k9 (4-8-11-6), work 18 st patt rep row 2 Chart A 4 (5-5-5-6) times, k9 (4-8-11-6).

Cont working rows 3–46 given for Chart A, followed by rows 1–46 given for Chart B in sequence as set. Work in this way (rows 1–46 Chart A, followed by rows 1–46 Chart B) throughout until piece measures 13.5 (14-14-14.5-15.5) in [34 (35.5-35.5-37-39) cm] from beg, end with RS row facing for next row.

shape armholes as follows:
Cont in patt and sequence, BO 2 (2-3-3-3) sts at beg of next 4 rows, 82 (90-94-100-108) sts rem. Work even in patt until piece measures 7 (7-7-7.5-7.5) in [18 (18-18-19-19) cm] from beg of armhole shaping, end RS row facing for next row.

shape back neck as follows:
Cont in patt work across 22 (26-28-30-32) sts, turn (this is neck edge). Leave rem 60 (64-66-70-76) sts on a spare needle. Working on the 22 (26-28-30-32) sts

only, dec 1 st at neck edge on next 4 rows, 18 (22-24-26-28) sts. Work WS row even.

shape shoulder as follows:

cont in patt BO 6 (7-8-9-9) sts at beg of next row. Work WS row even. Rep last 2 rows once more. BO rem 6 (8-8-8-10) sts.

Return to sts on spare needle. Slip center 38 (38-38-40-44) sts onto a stitch holder. Rejoin yarn to rem 22 (26-28-30-32) sts and patt to end. Dec 1 st at neck edge on next 4 rows, 18 (22-24-26-28) sts. Work 2 rows even.

shape shoulder as follows:

Cont in patt BO 6 (7-8-9-9) sts at beg of next row. Work RS row even. Rep last 2 rows once more. BO rem 6 (8-8-8-10) sts.

FRONT

Work as given for back until armhole shaping has been completed.

Work even until piece measures 4.5 (4.5-4.5-5-5) in [11.5 (11.5-11.5-12.5-12.5) cm] from beg of armhole shaping.

shape front neck as follows:

Cont in patt work across 36 (40-42-44-46) sts, turn (this is neck edge). Leave rem 46 (50-52-56-62) sts on a spare needle. Working on the 36 (40-42-44-46) sts only, dec 1 st at neck edge on next 18 rows, 18 (22-24-26-28) sts. Work even until piece measures the same as back before shoulder shaping, end RS row facing for next row.

shape shoulder as follows:

Cont in patt BO 6 (7-8-9-9) sts at beg of next row. Work WS row even. Rep last 2 rows once more. BO rem 6 (8-8-8-10) sts.

Return to sts on spare needle. Slip center 10 (10-10-12-16) sts onto a stitch holder. Rejoin yarn to rem 36 (40-42-44-46) sts, patt to end. Dec 1 st at neck edge on next 18 rows, 18 (22-24-26-28) sts. Work even until piece measures the same as back before shoulder shaping, end WS row facing for next row.

shape shoulder as follows:

Cont in patt BO 6 (7-8-9-9) sts at beg of next row. Work RS row even. Rep last 2 rows once more. BO rem 6 (8-8-8-10) sts.

SLEEVE (MAKE 2 ALIKE)

Using 5 mm needles, cast on 60 sts. Work 3 rows in seed stitch, then place pattern as follows:

RS: p3, (work 18 st patt rep row 1 Chart A) 3 times, p3.

WS: k3, (work 18 st patt rep row 2 Chart A) 3 times, k3.

Cont working rows 3–46 given for Chart A, followed by rows 1–46 given for Chart B in sequence as set. Work in this way (rows 1–46 Chart A, followed by rows 1–46 Chart B) throughout, *at the same time* inc 1 st at each end of row 7 (7-7-9-9) and then every following 8th (8-8-6-6) row 9 (9-9-12-12) times, 80 (80-80-86-86) sts, take all incs

sts into rev St St. *Note:* place markers to designate beg chart placements to help keep track of increases.

Work even in patt until sleeve measures 13.5 (13.5-13.5-14-14) in [34 (34-34-35.5-35.5) cm] from beg.

shape cap as follows:

Cont in patt BO 6 sts at beg of next 10 rows. BO rem 20 (20-20-26-26) sts.

FINISHING AND NECK

Weave in ends. Block all pieces to given dimensions. Join RHS shoulder seam.

Using 5 mm needles, beg at LHS shoulder with RS facing, pick up and knit 28 sts down LHS of front neck, knit 10 (10-10-12-16) sts from front neck stitch holder, then pick up and knit 28 sts up RHS of front neck, pick up and knit 10 sts down RHS back neck, knit 38 (38-38-40-44) sts from back neck stitch holder, then pick up and knit 10 sts up LHS back neck, 124 (124-124-128-136) sts total. Work 2 rows in seed st. BO in patt.

Set in sleeves to armholes. Sew side and sleeve seams. Press lightly following the instructions on the yarn label.

mindfulness pointer: unplug and connect with friends

Almost everybody I knew spoke about the blackout of 2003 with delight: it was exciting and a bit fun, despite the huge inconvenience. It sparked impromptu parties and challenged the ingenuity of people who are used to simply pushing a button to make something work. Being disconnected from the grid brought about an increased sense of connection, causing people to work together, to share, and to offer help; these are the human values we long for most in life, especially us city-dwellers. It became clear to many of us that our abundant electrical supply seems to disconnect us from people as much as it connects us.

Knitting doesn't always have to be a solitary activity; meeting with friends while you work on projects is fun. When you knit in public places, you invariably start chatting with someone. So why not use this project to meet with knitting friends, unplugged?

inspired by time

WE OFTEN LONG FOR A RETURN TO TRADITION AS AN ANTIDOTE TO A FAST-PACED LIFE, BUT THAT DOESN'T MEAN OUR CLOTHING CAN'T BE FASHIONABLE AND CURRENT. CABLE-KNIT SWEATERS CAN PRO-VIDE A CLASSIC, TIMELESS LOOK WITH A MODERN TWIST THAT APPEALS TO TODAY'S KNITTERS, WHO WILL BE AMPLY REWARDED FOR THE TIME THEY DEVOTE TO A PROJECT.

Our most precious commodity, next to love, may well be time. We all yearn to have more time, either to get more work done, to spend with friends and family, to participate in favorite hobbies, or to just relax. Time may be a man-made invention, simply a tool for measure-ment, but it is a powerful force in our lives. The power of time is curi-ous; when we are fully engrossed in doing something we love, time is the last thing on our minds.

Most of us are fascinated by what is new and what is current, but fashion is constantly borrowing from a previous age. When we make a clothing purchase involving a hefty price tag, most times we will select something with classic, timeless appeal. The same is true for a knitted project; if you are going to invest a large chunk of time into making something by hand, you hope that it will remain a favorite for some time to come. I made this a major consideration when I designed these garments. I thought about the classic garments we wear over and over; then I borrowed from these favorites and gave them a twist to keep them looking modern.

ripples in time

All actions produce a ripple effect, like dropping a stone into water. These effects can transcend time and travel to realms far removed from the source of the action. I realize that maybe I will never see or know the effects of the ripples that I set in motion. But if I approach my actions with the intention of bringing joy, I hope that the effects of my ripples will carry that thought with them.

As I witness global events unfolding, I always find myself wondering how what I do can possibly matter in the larger scheme of things. I am not a brain surgeon, a political leader, or even particularly radical in my thinking, so how can my work make a difference? But in conversations with the mentors that I have surrounded myself with, I have come to the conclusion that I have to follow the course that my talents take me on, trusting that I will leave good things in my wake.

Through my work, I may encourage people to knit and enjoy the relaxation it brings, making them calmer, more focused partners, parents, employees or friends. I may even ignite a spark of curiosity that leads them to viewing the world a bit differently. I will never know for sure, but that's okay.

The occasion of the birth of a new human being is a hopeful time brimming with potential. We will watch with wonder as this tiny life grows and develops into a unique individual. With this in mind, I sought to infuse this sweater—to be worn in someone's first few weeks of life—with a cable pattern that speaks to the ripples set in motion by the advent of a new life.

SIZES / FINISHED CHEST MEASUREMENTS

19 in [48 cm]
21 in [53 cm]
25 in [63.5 cm]
27 in [68.5 cm]

Instructions are given for smallest size. If changes are necessary for larger sizes, the instructions are given in ( ). Where there is only one set of figures, this applies to all sizes.

MATERIALS

Baby Ull Dalegarn by Dale of Norway, shade 9013, 4 (4-5-5) balls, (100% wool).

Pair of 3 mm needles, CN, 2 stitch holders.

Yarn amounts given are based on average requirements and are approximate.

TENSION / GAUGE

36 sts and 44 rows = 4 in [10 cm] over cable pattern.

Take the time to check your gauge; change needle sizes if necessary to obtain correct gauge and garment size.

REFER TO GLOSSARY ON PAGE 13 FOR: SEED STITCH, REVERSE STOCKINETTE STITCH.

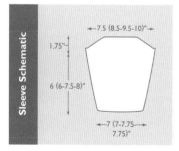

Sleeve Schematic

←7.5 (8.5-9.5-10)"→

1.75"

6 (6-7.5-8)"

←7 (7-7.75-7.75)"→

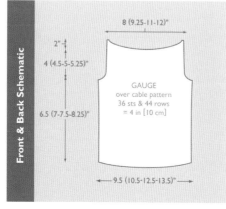

Front & Back Schematic

8 (9.25-11-12)"

2"

4 (4.5-5-5.25)"

GAUGE
over cable pattern
36 sts & 44 rows
= 4 in [10 cm]

6.5 (7-7.5-8.25)"

←9.5 (10.5-12.5-13.5)"→

Symbols Used in These Charts

- ⊡ p on RS; k on WS
- ☐ k on RS; p on WS
- C4B
- C4F
- T4B
- T4F

Chart A

Chart reads R to L RS rows and L to R WS rows

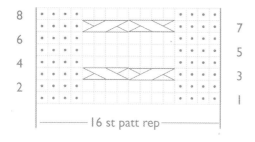

8
6
4
2
7
5
3
1

— 16 st patt rep —

Chart B

Chart reads R to L RS rows and L to R WS rows

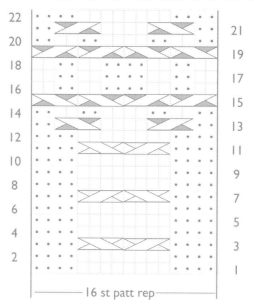

22
20
18
16
14
12
10
8
6
4
2
21
19
17
15
13
11
9
7
5
3
1

— 16 st patt rep —

Please see note on placing markers in
Things You Need to Know Before You Begin (p.8)

PATTERN A

Row 1 (RS): p4, k8, p4.

Row 2: k4, p8, k4.

Row 3: p4, C4B, C4F, p4.

Rows 4–6: rep row 2, then rep rows 1 and 2 once more.

Row 7: p4, C4F, C4B, p4.

Row 8: rep row 2.

Rep rows 1–8 for patt A.

PATTERN B

Row 1 (RS): p4, k8, p4.

Row 2: k4, p8, k4.

Row 3: p4, C4B, C4F, p4.

Rows 4–6: rep row 2, then rows 1 and 2 once more.

Row 7: p4, C4F, C4B, p4.

Rows 8–12: rep row 2, then rows 1–4 once more.

Row 13: p2, T4B, k4, T4F, p2.

Row 14: k2, p2, k2, p4, k2, p2, k2.

Row 15: (T4B) twice, (T4F) twice.

Row 16: p2, k2, p2, k4, p2, k2, p2.

Row 17: k2, p2, k2, p4, k2, p2, k2.

Row 18: rep row 16.

Row 19: (T4F) twice, (T4B) twice.

Row 20: rep row 14.

Row 21: p2, T4F, k4, T4B, p2.

Row 22: rep row 2.

Rep rows 1–22 for patt B.

BACK AND FRONT
(ALIKE)

Using 3 mm needles, cast on 86 (96-112-122) sts. Work 1 row in seed st, then place pattern as follows:

RS row: p3 (8-0-5) (work 16 st patt rep row 1 Chart A, then work 16 st patt rep row 1 Chart B) 2 (2-3-3) times, then work 16 st patt rep Chart A once more, p3 (8-0-5).

WS row: k3 (8-0-5) (work 16 st patt rep row 2 Chart A, then work 16 st patt rep row 2 Chart B) 2 (2-3-3) times, then work 16 st patt rep Chart A once more, k3 (8-0-5).

Cont working chart rows in sequence as set until piece measures 6.5 (7-7.5-8.25) in [16.5 (18-19-21) cm] from beg, end RS row facing for next row.

shape armholes as follows:

Cont working in patt, BO 3 sts at beg of next 4 rows, 74 (84-100-110) sts rem. Work even until piece measures 4 (4.5-5-5.25) in [10 (11.5-12.5-13) cm] from beg of armhole shaping, end RS row facing for next row.

shape neckline as follows:

Cont in patt work across 30 (33-42-48) sts, turn (this is neck edge). Leave rem 44 (51-58-62) sts on a spare needle. Working on the 30 (33-42-48) sts only, BO 4 (5-8-10) sts at beg of WS row, work to end in patt. Work RS row even in patt. Rep the last 2 rows twice more, 18 sts rem. Cont in patt, dec 1 st at neck edge on next 15 rows, p3tog, break off yarn and draw through loop.

Return to sts on spare needle. Slip center 14 (18-16-14) sts onto a stitch holder. Rejoin yarn to rem 30 (33-42-48) sts. BO 4 (5-8-10) sts at beg of this row, work to end in patt. Work WS row even in patt. Rep the last 2 rows twice more, 18 sts rem. Cont in patt,

dec 1 st at neck edge on next 15 rows, k3tog, break off yarn and draw through loop.

SLEEVE (MAKE 2 ALIKE)

Using 3 mm needles, cast on 64 (64-70-70) sts. Work 1 row in seed stitch, then place pattern as follows:

RS row: p0 (0-3-3), (work 16 st patt rep row 1 Chart A) 4 times, p0 (0-3-3).

WS row: k0 (0-3-3), (work 16 st patt rep row 2 Chart A) 4 times, k0 (0-3-3).

Cont working chart rows in sequence as set, *at the same time* inc 1 st at each end of row 21 (9-9-7) and then every following 22th (10-10-8) row 1 (3-4-9) times, 68 (72-80-90) sts. Then inc 1 st at each end of every following 0th (8-8-0) row 0 (2-3-0) times, 68 (76-86-90) sts. Work all incs sts into rev St St. Then work even in patt until sleeve measures 6 (6-7.5-8) in [15.25 (15.25-19-20) cm] from beg, end RS row facing for next row.

shape cap as follows:

Cont in patt BO 3 (3-4-4) sts at beg of next 2 rows, and 3 (3-5-5) sts at beg of following 2 rows.

Then dec 1 st at each end of next 10 rows. Then BO 4 (6-7-8) sts at beg of next 4 rows. BO rem 20 sts.

FINISHING AND NECK

Working on 1st piece, using 3 mm needles, with RS facing pick up and knit 38 (38-40-42) sts down side of neck, work across 14 (18-16-14) sts from stitch holder, then pick up and knit 38 (38-40-42) sts up other side of neck, 90 (94-96-98) sts total. Work 3 rows in seed st. BO in patt.

Rep for other body piece.

Block all pieces to given dimensions. Place markers on both armholes 2.5 (3-3.5-3.75) in [6.25 (7.5-9-9.5) cm] up from beg of armhole shaping on both pieces (4 markers). Overlap neck extensions front to back so that points touch the markers, ensure that both sides overlap in the same direction, pin in place. Sew in sleeve to armholes working through both layers at neck extensions.

Sew side and sleeve seams. Press lightly, following the instructions on the yarn label.

mindfulness pointer: gift of time

We all have a finite amount of time, so it is a loving gesture to use some of this most precious commodity to make something for somebody else. The same is also true when we make something for ourselves—it says we are worth the effort. Make this sweater for a baby born to a friend, a relative, or somebody that you don't even know. Babies will feel the love of another person by wearing something handcrafted in their first few weeks of life. They instinctively feel the love in each stitch and are comforted by it, a great experience at the start of life.

evolving traditions

Most families create their own traditions to mark holidays and celebrations. But the traditions that we cling to are always evolving, just as our families themselves are always changing.

Sometimes changes take place slowly and are hardly perceived. Others are more dramatic, and when they occur they cause us to create brand-new traditions, simply because it is no longer possible to continue with what has gone before. After a birth, a new individual has to be accommodated; after a death, a missing loved one must be mourned and remembered; after a union, two sets of traditions have to be melded together.

In much the same way, fashions either evolve gradually over time or they change radically due to the advent of a new fiber or a sociological shift in views.

As a knitter, I am acutely aware of the traditions present in the craft, which slowly become ingrained in our psyche through the act of repetition. We are linked—both to the past and to those yet to discover our craft—by the thread of current practice. We are part of a continuum. When designing, I strive to acknowledge the history while pushing the craft forward and keeping it relevant in our contemporary world.

In designing this sweater, I wanted to pay homage to the traditions of knitting. So I incorporated Fair Isle patterning along with the cables. Then I included a textured pattern made by simple knit and purl stitches—the foundations on which all knitting patterns are built. The cables I selected move gently and smoothly to reflect our desire to keep some kind of control over inevitable changes.

SIZES / FINISHED CHEST
MEASUREMENTS

Small 36.5 in [93 cm]
Medium 38 in [96.5 cm]
Large 40 in [101.5 cm]
XL 42 in [106.5 cm]
2X 44 in [112 cm]

Instructions are given for smallest size. If changes are necessary for larger sizes, the instructions are given in ( ). Where there is only one set of figures, this applies to all sizes.

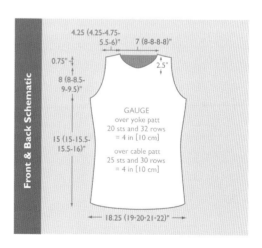

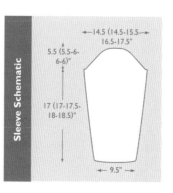

MATERIALS

Alpaca Merino by Sweaterkits, (40% alpaca–60% merino)

M/C: shade Camel, 7(7-8-9-10) 50 g balls.

Color A: shade Cream, 5 (5-6-6-7) 50 g balls.

Color B: shade Chestnut, 1 x 50 g balls.

Pair of 4 mm needles, pair of 3.75 mm needles, 16 in [40 cm]-long 3.75 mm circular needle and 16 in [40 cm]-long 4 mm circular needle required for neck, CN, 6 stitch holders.

Yarn amounts given are based on average requirements and are approximate.

TENSION / GAUGE

25 sts and 30 rows = 4 in [10 cm] over cable pattern with 4 mm needles.

20 sts and 32 = 4 in [10 cm] over yoke/ sleeve pattern with 3.75 mm needles.

Take the time to check your gauge; change needle sizes if necessary to obtain correct gauge and garment size.

REFER TO TECHNIQUES ON PAGE 12 FOR: SHORT ROWS, 3-NEEDLE BIND OFF, FAIR ISLE TECHNIQUE.

Symbols Used in These Charts

⊡	p on RS; k on WS	◪	T2B	◪	T3B	◪	C4B	◪	T4B
☐	k on RS; p on WS	◪	T2F	◪	T3F	◪	C4F	◪	T4F
☐	PB								

Chart A

Chart reads R to L RS rows and L to R WS rows

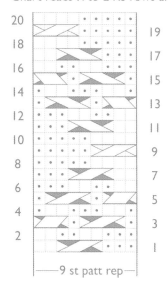

└─ 9 st patt rep ─┘

Chart B

Chart reads R to L RS rows and L to R WS rows

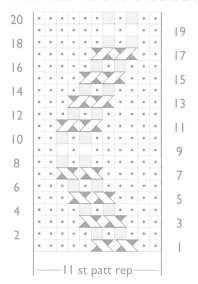

└─ 11 st patt rep ─┘

Chart C

Chart reads R to L RS rows and L to R WS rows

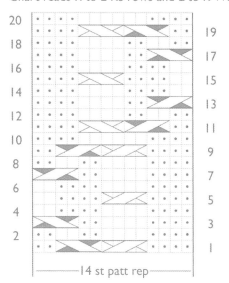

└─ 14 st patt rep ─┘

Chart D

Chart reads R to L RS rows and L to R WS rows

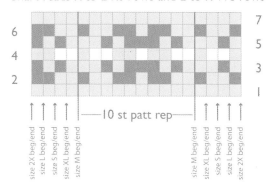

└─ 10 st patt rep ─┘

size 2X beg/end
size L beg/end
size S beg/end
size XL beg/end
size M beg/end

size M beg/end
size XL beg/end
size S beg/end
size L beg/end
size 2X beg/end

Chart Color Key

☐ M/C

☐ A

■ B

PATTERN A

Row 1 (RS): p3, T4B, k2.

Row 2: p2, k2, p2, k3.

Row 3: p1, T4B, p1, T3B.

Row 4: k1, p2, k3, p2, k1.

Row 5: T3B, p1, T4B, p1.

Row 6: k3, p2, k2, p2.

Row 7: k2, T4B, p3.

Row 8: k5, p4.

Row 9: C4B, p5.

Row 10: k5, p4.

Row 11: k2, T4F, p3.

Row 12: rep row 6.

Row 13: T3F, p1, T4F, p1.

Row 14: rep row 4.

Row 15: p1, T4F, p1, T3F.

Row 16: rep row 2.

Row 17: p3, T4F, k2.

Row 18: p4, k5.

Row 19: p5, C4B.

Row 20: p4, k5.

Rep Rows 1–20 for patt A.

PATTERN B

Row 1 (RS): p2, (T2F) twice, p5.

Row 2: k5, PB1, k1, PB1, k3.

Row 3: p3, (T2F) twice, p4.

Row 4: k4, PB1, k1, PB1, k4.

Row 5: p4, (T2F) twice, p3.

Row 6: k3, PB1, k1, PB1, k5.

Row 7: p5, (T2F) twice, p2.

Row 8: k2, PB1, k1, PB1, k6.

Row 9: p6, k1, p1, k1, p2.

Row 10: rep row 8.

Row 11: p5, (T2B) twice, p2.

Row 12: rep row 6.

Row 13: p4, (T2B) twice, p3.

Row 14: rep row 4.

Row 15: p3, (T2B) twice, p4.

Row 16: rep row 2.

Row 17: p2, (T2B) twice, p5.

Row 18: k6, PB1, k1, PB1, k2.

Row 19: p2, k1, p1, k1, p6.

Row 20: rep row 18.

Rep rows 1–20 for patt B.

PATTERN C

Row 1 (RS): p4, C4B, T4F, p2.

Row 2: k2, p2, k2, p4, k4.

Row 3: p4, k4, p2, T4F.

Row 4: p2, k4, p4, k4.

Row 5: p4, C4B, p4, k2.

Row 6: rep row 4.

Row 7: p4, k4, p2, T4B.

Row 8: k2, p2, k2, p4, k4.

Row 9: p4, C4B, T4B, p2.

Row 10: k4, p6, k4.

Row 11: p2, T4B, C4F, p4.

Row 12: k4, p4, k2, p2, k2.

Row 13: T4B, p2, k4, p4.

Row 14: k4, p4, k4, p2.

Row 15: k2, p4, C4F, p4.

Row 16: rep row 14.

Row 17: T4F, p2, k4, p4.

Row 18: rep row 12.

Row 19: p2, T4F, C4F, p4.

Row 20: rep row 10.

Rep rows 1–20 for patt C.

SLEEVE/YOKE PATTERN

Row 1 (RS): p2 (0-3-1-0), *k2, p2, k3, p2, rep from * to last 4 (2-5-3-2) sts, k2, p2 (0-3-1-0).

Rows 2 and 4: purl all sts.

Row 3: p2 (0-3-1-0), *k2, p7, rep from * to last 4 (2-5-3-2) sts, k2, p2 (0-3-1-0).

Rep rows 1–4 for patt.

BACK

Using 4 mm needles and M/C, cast on 114 (120-126-132-138) sts. Work set-up rows as follows:

RS set up: p8 (11-14-17-20), k4, p2, k1, p1, k1, p11, k4, p2, k1, p1, k1, p10, k6, p8, k6, p6, k1, p1, k1, p11, k4, p2, k1, p1, k1, p11, k4, p3 (6-9-12-15).

WS set up: k3 (6-9-12-15), p4, k11, p1, k1, p1, k2, p4, k11, p1, k1, p1, k6, p6, k8, p6, k10, p1, k1, p1, k2, p4, k11, p1, k1, p1, k2, p4, k8 (11-14-17-20).

place cable panels as follows:

Panels are mirrored at the center point, like so: rev St St-A-B-A-B-C/C-B-A-B-A-rev St St

Row 1: (work as given row 1 of each chart) p3 (6-9-12-15), (work 9 st patt rep Chart A, then work 11 st patt rep Chart B) twice, (work 14 st patt rep Chart C) twice, (work 11 st patt rep Chart B, then work 9 st patt rep Chart A) twice, p3 (6-9-12-15).

Row 2: (work as given for row 2 of each chart) k3 (6-9-12-15), (work 9 st patt rep Chart A, then work 11 st patt rep Chart B) twice, (work 14 st patt rep Chart C) twice, (work 11 st patt rep Chart B, then work 9 st patt rep as given Chart A) twice, k3 (6-9-12-15).

Cont working chart rows in sequence as set, until work measures 4 (3.5-3.75-3.75-4) in [10 (9-9.5-9.5-10) cm] from beg.

shape waist as follows:

Cont in patt, dec 1 st at each end of next row, work 7 rows even in patt. Rep last 8 rows 1 (2-2-2-2) more times, then dec row again,

108 (112-118-124-130) sts rem. Work 11 rows even in patt.

Cont in patt inc 1 st at each end of next row, work 7 rows even in patt, rep last 8 rows 1 (2-2-2-2) more times, then inc row again, 114 (120-126-132-138) sts.

Cont working even in patt until piece measures 15 (15-15.5-15.5-16) in [38 (38-38-39-39-40.5) cm] from beg, end RS row facing for next row.

shape armholes as follows:

Cont in patt, BO 5 sts at beg of next 2 rows. Then dec 1 st at each end of next 6 rows. Then dec 1 st at each end of next 4 RS rows, 84 (90-96-102-108) sts rem. Work 7 rows even, end with RS row facing for next row.

Change to Color B, knit 2 rows (garter ridge). Now working in Fair Isle technique, follow rows 1–7 Chart D beg/end as indicated for size and changing colors where indicated.

Then using Color B, purl 2 rows, dec 6 (7-7-8-7) sts evenly across 2nd row, 78 (83-89-94-101) sts rem.

Change to Color A and to 3.75 mm needles, beg with row 2 of patt work in Sleeve/Yoke patt until armhole measures 8 (8-8.5-9-9.5) in [20 (20-21.5-23-24) cm] from beg of shaping, end having just worked row 1 of patt.

shape shoulders as follows:

Cont in patt throughout:

Next row: work to last 7 (7-8-9-10) sts, wrap next st, turn, leave rem sts unworked in hold for shoulder. WS row: rep last row.

Next row: work to last 14 (14-16-18-20) sts, wrap next st, turn. Rep this row.

Next row: work to last 21 (21-24-27-30) sts, wrap next st, turn. Rep this row. Place each set of sts for shoulders onto separate stitch holders and center 36 (41-41-40-41) sts onto another stitch holder for back neck.

FRONT

Work as given for back until work measures 5.5 (5.5-6-6.5-7) in [14 (14-15-16.5-18) cm] from beg of armhole shaping, ending having just worked row 2 of patt, RS row facing for next row.

shape front neck as follows:

Cont in patt throughout, work across 33 (36-39-42-45) sts, turn (this is neck edge), leave rem 45 (47-50-52-56) sts on a spare needle. Working on the 33 (36-39-42-45) sts only, work WS row even.

RS row: work across 31 (33-36-39-42) sts, wrap next st, turn, leave rem sts unworked in hold for front neck. Work WS row even.

RS row: work across 29 (31-34-37-40) sts, wrap next st, turn. Work WS row even.

RS row: work across 28 (29-32-35-38) sts, wrap next st, turn. Work WS row even.

RS row: work across 27 (27-30-33-36) sts, wrap next st, turn.

Slip 6 (9-9-9-9) sts in hold onto a stitch holder. Then working on rem 27 (27-30-33-36) sts dec 1 st at neck edge on next 6 rows, 21 (21-24-27-30) rem, work even until piece measures the same as back before shoulder shaping, end with WS row facing for next row.

shape shoulder as follows:

WS row: work to last 7 (7-8-9-10) sts, wrap next st, turn, leave rem sts unworked in hold for shoulder. Work RS even.

Next row: work to last 14 (14-16-18-20) sts, wrap next st, turn. Work RS even.

Place 21 (21-24-27-30) sts for shoulder onto a st holder.

Return to sts on spare needle. Slip center 12 (11-11-10-11) sts onto the same st holder used for 6 (9-9-9-9) sts in hold from LHS front neck, rejoin yarn and work across rem 33 (36-39-42-45) sts.

WS row: work across 31 (33-36-39-42) sts, wrap next st, turn. Work RS row even.

WS row: work across 29 (31-34-37-40) sts, wrap next st, turn. Work RS row even.

WS row: work across 28 (29-32-35-38) sts, wrap next st, turn.

Work RS row even.

WS row: work across 27 (27-30-33-36) sts, wrap next st, turn.

Slip 6 (9-9-9-9) sts in hold onto same front neck stitch holder. Then working on rem 27 (27-30-33-36) sts dec 1 st at neck edge on next 6 rows, 21 (21-24-27-30) sts rem, work even until piece measures the same as back before shoulder shaping, end RS row facing for next row.

shape shoulder as follows:

RS row: work to last 7 (7-8-9-10) sts, wrap next st, turn, leave rem sts unworked in hold for shoulder. Work WS even.

Next row: work to last 14 (14-16-18-20) sts, wrap next st, turn. Work WS even.

Place 21 (21-24-27-30) sts for shoulder onto a st holder.

SLEEVE (MAKE 2 ALIKE)

Using 3.75 mm needles and Color A, cast on 47 sts and work in Sleeve/Yoke pattern as given for 2nd size, *at the same time* inc 1 st at each end of row 11 (11-13-3-7)

and every following 10th (10-8-8-8-8) row 9 (9-14-14-8) more times, 67 (67-77-77-65) sts. Then inc 1 st at each end of every following 8th (8-0-6-6) row 3 (3-0-3-11) times, 73 (73-77-83-87) sts, take all inc sts into pattern as appropriate. Then work even in patt until sleeve measures 17 (17-17.5-18-18.5) in [43 (43-44.5-45.5-47) cm] from beg.

shape cap as follows:

Cont in patt, BO 5 sts at beg of next 2 rows. Then dec 1 st at beg of following 20 (20-22-22-23) RS rows, 23 (23-23-29-31) sts rem. BO 4 (4-4-7-8) sts at beg of next 2 rows. BO rem 15 sts.

FINISHING AND NECKLINE

Weave in all ends. Block all pieces to given dimensions.

Join both shoulder seams using the 3-needle BO method.

With RS facing, using 3.75 mm circular needle and Color A, beg at RHS shoulder seam, work across 36 (41-41-40-41) sts from back neck stitch holder in patt,

then pick up and knit 14 (10-14-15-19) sts down LHS front neck, knit across 24 (29-29-28-29) sts from front neck stitch holder, picking up wraps and inc 2 (0-1-1-0) sts evenly across these sts, then pick up and knit 14 (10-14-15-19) sts up RHS front neck, 90 (90-99-99-108) sts total.

Place marker to indicate first st of each rnd, work in rnds lining up patt as appropriate.

Rnd 1: knit all sts.

Rnd 2: work 9 st rep row 3 of Sleeve/Yoke patt.

Rnd 3: knit all sts.

Rnd 4: work 9 st rep row 1 of Sleeve/Yoke patt.

Rep these rnds 4 more times. Knit 1 rnd. Change to 4 mm circular needle, work next row as follows: (k2, inc in next st by working into st twice) rep to end, 120 (120-132-132-144) sts. Purl next rnd. BO loosely knitwise.

Set in sleeves to armholes. Sew side and sleeve seams. Press lightly, following the instructions on the yarn label.

mindfulness pointer: threading traditions together

Do you feel a difference when working the three stitch patterns: the softly undulating movement of the cables, the excitement and punctuation of the Fair Isle pattern, the steady rhythm of the knit and purl stitch? While you work each body piece, think about how you are exploring Fair Isle and cable-knitting traditions, culminating in the simplicity of a knit-and-purl-textured pattern at the yoke, like returning to the roots of knitting history.

metro retro

Fashion is constantly borrowing from the history books. Sometimes it simply flips back a page, other times it skips back a few chapters, and often it jumps to an earlier volume.

How people dress can tell us a lot about an era. Contrast the forward-thinking, break-the-rules attitude of 1960s fashions with that of our current age, which constantly borrows from decades past.

This nostalgia for a bygone age influences all areas of fashion. If it isn't the actual clothes that hark back to earlier days, then it's the accessories, which might include a piece of jewelry that came from our grandmother's box, or at least looks like it could have. Even movie stars are wearing vintage gowns on award nights.

This men's project drew its inspiration from the trend for designing sports gear with a retro feel. Watching a hockey game sparked the inspiration for this sweater. I was attracted to the redesign of my local team's uniforms, developed from a vintage kit. I loved the styling and thought that something similar would look great as a man's sweater. I changed the color placements, but kept with a color-block feel to further reference the sporty look.

SIZES / FINISHED CHEST MEASUREMENTS

Small 44 in [112 cm]

Medium 48 in [122 cm]

Large 53 in [134.5 cm]

XL 58 in [147 cm]

Instructions are given for smallest size. If changes are necessary for larger sizes, the instructions are given in ( ). Where there is only one set of figures, this applies to all sizes.

MATERIALS

18/24 wool by Mission Falls, (100% wool).

Color A: shade 010 Russet, 11 (12-13-15) 50 g balls.

Color B: shade 013 Curry, 7 (8-9-10) 50 g balls.

Pair of 4.5 mm needles, 4 stitch holders, CN.

Yarn amounts given are based on average requirements and are approximate.

TENSION / GAUGE

20 sts and 26 rows = 4 in [10 cm] over textured knit and purl body pattern.

27 sts and 26 rows over cable panel.

Take the time to check your gauge; change needle sizes if necessary to obtain correct gauge and garment size.

REFER TO GLOSSARY ON PAGE 13 FOR: SEED STITCH, AND TO TECHNIQUES ON PAGE 12 FOR: 3-NEEDLE BO.

Sleeve Schematic

17.5 (17.5-19-19.25)"

3.25 (3-3.75-4)

2.5 (3.75-3.75-4.5)

7 (7-7.75-8)"

17.75 (18.5-18.5-19)"

← 10.5" →

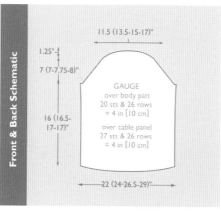

Front & Back Schematic

11.5 (13.5-15-17)"

1.25"

7 (7-7.75-8)"

GAUGE
over body patt
20 sts & 26 rows
= 4 in [10 cm]

over cable panel
27 sts & 26 rows
= 4 in [10 cm]

16 (16.5-17-17)"

22 (24-26.5-29)"

Symbols Used in These Charts

⊡ p on RS; k on WS   ⬛ C4B   ⬛ T4B

☐ k on RS; p on WS   ⬛ T4F

Chart A

Chart reads R to L RS rows and L to R WS rows

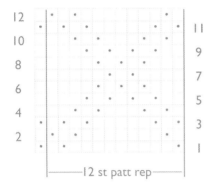

├─12 st patt rep─┤

Chart B

Chart reads R to L RS rows and L to R WS rows

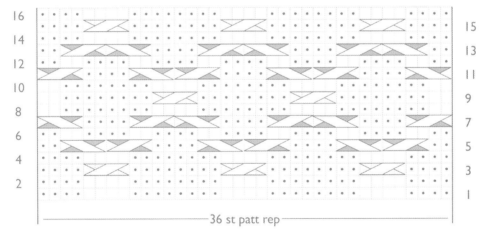

├─────36 st patt rep─────┤

Please see note on placing markers in Things You Need to Know Before You Begin (p.8)

PATTERN A

Row 1 (RS): *p1, k9, p1, k1, rep from * to last st, p1.

Row 2: p1, *k1, p1, k1, p7, k1, p1, rep from * to end.

Row 3: *p1, k1, p1, k5, (p1, k1) twice, rep from * to last st, p1.

Row 4: p1, *p2, k1, p1, k1, p3, (k1, p1) twice, rep from * to end.

Row 5: *k2, (p1, k1) 3 times, p1, k3, rep from *to last st, k1.

Row 6: p1, *p4, (k1, p1) twice, k1, p3, rep from * to end.

Row 7: *k4, p1, k1, p1, k5, rep from * to last st, k1.

Row 8: rep row 6.

Row 9: rep row 5.

Row 10: rep row 4.

Row 11: rep row 3.

Row 12: rep row 2.

Rep rows 1–12 for patt A.

PATTERN B

Row 1 (RS): p4, (k4, p8) twice, k4, p4.

Row 2: k4, (p4, k8) twice, p4, k4.

Row 3: p4, (C4B, p8) twice, C4B, p4.

Row 4: rep row 2.

Row 5: p2, (T4B, T4F, p4) twice, T4B, T4F, p2.

Row 6: k2, (p2, k4) 5 times, p2, k2.

Row 7: (T4B, p4, T4F) 3 times.

Row 8: p2, (k8, p4) twice, k8, p2.

Row 9: k2, (p8, C4B) twice, p8, k2.

Row 10: rep row 8.

Row 11: (T4F, p4, T4B) 3 times.

Row 12: rep row 6.

Row 13: p2, (T4F, T4B, p4) twice, T4F, T4B, p2.

Row 14: rep row 2.

Row 15: rep row 3.

Row 16: rep row 2.

Rep rows 1–16 for patt B.

BACK AND FRONT (ALIKE)

Using Color A and 4.5 mm needles cast on 109 (121-133-145) sts and work 2 rows in seed st. Then place patt as follows:

Row 1 (RS): work 12 st patt rep Chart A 9 (10-11-12) times, 1 st rem, work as given at LHS of chart.

Row 2: beg at LHS of Chart A, work first 1 st, then work 12 st patt rep 9 (10-11-12) times.

Cont working chart rows in sequence as set until piece measures 16 (16.5-17-17)in [40.5 (42-43-43)cm], end with RS row facing for next row.

shape raglans as follows:

Cont in patt, BO 5 sts at beg of next 2 rows. Then dec 1 st at each end of next 22 (22-24-25) RS rows, 55 (67-75-85) sts rem, place marker at each end of this row. Cont in patt, BO 2 sts at beg of next 2 rows, 3 sts at beg of following 2 rows, 6 sts at beg of following 2 rows and 6 (9-12-15) sts at beg of following 2 rows. BO rem 21 (27-29-33) sts.

SLEEVE (MAKE 2 ALIKE)

Using Color A and 4.5 mm needles cast on 60 sts, knit 3 rows.

Change to Color B and purl 1 row. Then place cable patt as follows:

RS: p12, work 36 st patt rep row 1 Chart B, p12.

WS: k12, work 36 st patt rep row 2 Chart B, k12.

Cont working chart rows in sequence as set, *at the same time* inc 1 st at each end of row 3, and then every following 4th row 0 (0-8-9) times, 62 (62-78-80) sts, take all inc sts in rev St St throughout. Then inc 1 st at each end of every following 6th row 18 (18-13-13) times, 98 (98-104-106) sts. Work even in patt until sleeve measures approx 17.75 (18.5-18.5-19) in [45 (47-47-48) cm] from beg, end row 5 (9-9-13) Chart B facing for next row.

shape raglans as follows:

Cont in patt as set, BO 5 (5-6-6) sts at beg of next 2 rows. Then dec 1 st at each end of RS rows 22 (22-24-25) times, 44 sts rem, place marker at each end of this row. Work even in patt for a further approx 2.5 (3.75-3.75-4.5) in [6.5 (9.5-9.5-11.5) cm].

For RH sleeve end row 3 (15-3-15) Chart B facing for next row.

For LH sleeve end row 2 (14-2-14) Chart B facing for next row.

RH sleeve: working in patt rows given below, *at the same time* shape front neck:

S and L: rows 3 and 4 Chart B, then rep rows 1–4 Chart B throughout shaping.

M and XL: rows 15 and 16 Chart B, then rep rows 1–4 Chart B throughout shaping.

***Next row**: work across 16 sts in patt (this is neck edge), leave rem 28 sts on a spare needle. Working on the 16 sts only, dec 1 st at neck edge on next 3 rows. Work even in patt on rem 13 sts for a further 18 (16-20-22) rows. Leave these sts on a stitch holder for CF yoke seam.

Return to sts on spare needle, slip center 10 sts onto a stitch holder. Work even on rem 18 sts even in patt for 18 (16-20-22) rows. Leave these sts on a st holder for CB yoke seam. ***

LH sleeve: working in patt rows given below, *at the same time* shape front neck:

S and L: rows 2–4 Chart B, then rep rows 1–4 Chart B throughout.

M and XL: rows 14–16 Chart B, then rep rows 1–4 Chart B throughout.

Work as given for RH sleeve from *** to ***.

FINISHING AND NECKBAND

Weave in ends. Block out pieces to given dimensions.

Using Color B and 4.5 mm needles, working with both sets of 18 sts from sleeve extension stitch holders, place RS tog then join CB yoke seam using the 3-needle BO method. Join both back raglan seams, including sewing sleeve extensions across curved upper edge of back, matching markers.

Using 4.5 mm needle and Color B, with RS facing pick up and knit 20 sts along RHS front neck, knit across 10 sts from sleeve stitch holder, then pick up and knit 36 sts along joined back neck, knit across 10 sts from sleeve stitch holder, then pick up and knit 20 sts along LHS front neck, 96 sts total. Working back and forth, beg with WS row, work 4 rows in seed st. Change to A purl 3 rows. BO purlwise.

Using Color B and 4.5 mm needles, working with both sets of 13 sts from sleeve extension stitch holders, join CF yoke seam using the 3-needle BO method. Leave neckband open at CF. Join both front raglan seams, including sewing sleeve extensions across curved upper edge of front, matching markers. Join side and sleeve seams. Press lightly, following the instructions on the yarn label.

mindfulness pointer: make an ephemeria journal

May I suggest taking a camera with you while you work on this project? Take snapshots of your surroundings to record the time you spent on it. You are creating a mini time-capsule. If this project is a gift for somebody, you can keep the pictures in a journal to show them when you present the gift. Even if it isn't a gift, you will have the pleasure of looking back and remembering this chapter in your life in the years to come. Or you may even help a historian in the future understand our current age.

celtic icon

Life in a monastery is slow, contemplative, and without many of life's luxuries. But one thing that is abundant is time. At first glance, it might seem that the way monks spend their time produces few tangible results. How do you measure the accomplishment of spiritual enlightenment, or the far-reaching effects of selfless acts of kindness? We find it difficult to understand because we are programmed to believe that only measurable output can be seen as achievement.

But in the case of monasteries that produced exquisite illuminated manuscripts, we do have something tangible to measure. Because of the quality of execution apparent in the final results, we do not even concern ourselves with the time it took to produce them. They are so wonderful, who cares how long it took to make them? These are painstaking works of art, and I imagine that the daily progress of their creation would have been almost imperceptible. You might sometimes feel like this when knitting.

This design incorporates a cable reminiscent of Celtic patterns, in homage to the artists who produced those exquisite manuscripts. As a way of making the project relevant in our contemporary world, I have juxtaposed the old with the new by selecting a style reminiscent of that modern-day classic, the hooded sweatshirt. The hood on this cardigan sweater also gives a nod to the hooded cloaks worn by monks. To reinforce the modern feel, I used denim colors so that the sweater could be worn with jeans.

SIZES / FINISHED CHEST
MEASUREMENTS

Small 37 in [94 cm]

Medium 41 in [104 cm]

Large 46 in [117 cm]

XL 50 in [127 cm]

2X 54 in [137 cm]

Instructions are given for smallest size. If changes are necessary for larger sizes, the instructions are given in ( ). Where there is only one set of figures, this applies to all sizes.

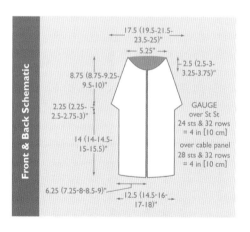

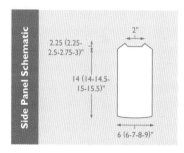

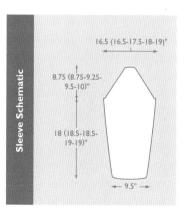

MATERIALS

Soft Touch wool/cotton blend by Shelridge Farm (85% wool–15% cotton)

M/C: shade denim, 4 (5-6-7-7) 100 g skeins.

Color A: shade sky blue, 2 (2-2-3-3) 100 g skeins.

Pair of 4 mm needles, 3 st holders, CN, 22-in[56 cm]-long separating zipper, sewing thread for attaching zipper.

TENSION / GAUGE

24 sts and 32 rows = 4 in [10 cm] over stockinette stitch.

28 sts and 32 rows = 4 in [10 cm] over cable panel (cable panel = 5 in [13 cm] wide).

Take the time to check your gauge; change needle sizes if necessary to obtain correct gauge and garment size.

SPECIAL INSTRUCTIONS

Work decs for raglan shapings 1 st in from selvage as follows:

RS rows: k1, k2togb, work to last 3 sts, k2tog, k1.

WS rows: p1, p2tog, work to last 3 sts, p2togb, p1.

Note: patt rep is 36 sts but incs to 44 sts during rows 7–18, when st count is noted in instructions cable panels are always counted as 36 sts.

REFER TO GLOSSARY ON PAGE 13 FOR: SEED STITCH, AND TO TECHNIQUES ON PAGE 12 FOR: BACK STITCH, WHIPSTITCH.

Symbols Used in This Chart

⊡	p on RS; k on WS	⊠	inc4	⬳	T3B	⬳	C4B	⬳	T4B
☐	k on RS; p on WS	⬿	dec4	⬳	T3F	⬳	C4F	⬳	T4F
▨	no stitch								

Chart reads R to L RS rows and L to R WS rows

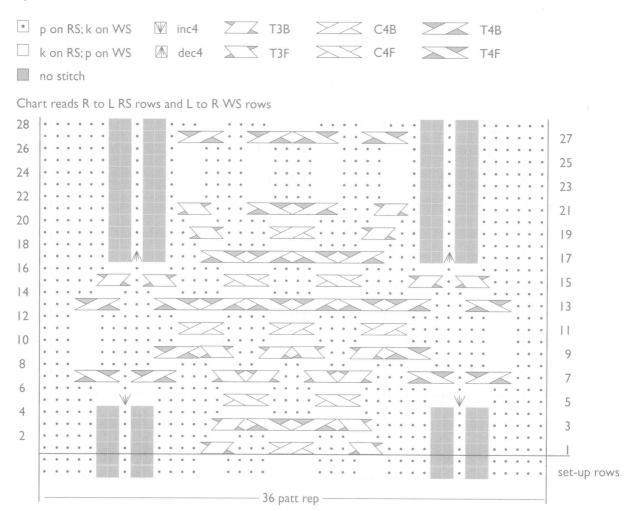

Note: beg 36 sts, inc to 44 sts rows 7–18, dec back to 36 sts rows 19–30

CABLE PATTERN

RS set-up row: p10, k2, p4, k4, p4, k2, p10.

WS set-up row: k10, p2, k4, p4, k4, p2, k10.

Row 1: p10, T3F, p3, C4B, p3, T3B, p10.

Row 2: k11, p2, k3, p4, k3, p2, k11.

Row 3: p11, T3F, T4B, T4F, T3B, p11.

Row 4: k12, p4, k4, p4, k12.

Row 5: p5, inc4, p6, C4F, p4, C4F, p6, inc4, p5, 44 sts.

Row 6: k5, p2, k1, p2, k6, p4, k4, p4, k6, p2, k1, p2, k5.

Row 7: p3, T4B, p1, T4F, p3, T3B, T3F, p2, T3B, T3F, p3, T4B, p1, T4F, p3.

Row 8: k3, p2, k5, p2, k3, (p2, k2) 3 times, p2, k3, p2, k5, p2, k3.

Row 9: p3, k2, p5, T4F, T3B, p2, T3F, T3B, p2, T3F, T4B, p5, k2, p3.

Row 10: k3, p2, k7, (p4, k4) twice, p4, k7, p2, k3.

Row 11: p3, k2, p7, (C4B, p4) twice, C4B, p7, k2, p3.

Row 12: rep row 10.

Row 13: p3, T4F, p3, T4B, (T4F, T4B) twice, T4F, p3, T4B, p3.

Row 14: k5, p2, k3, p2, (k4, p4) twice, k4, p2, k3, p2, k5.

Row 15: p5, T3F, p1, T3B, (p4, C4F) twice, p4, T3F, p1, T3B, p5.

Row 16: k6, p2, k1, p2, k5, p4, k4, p4, k5, p2, k1, p2, k6.

Row 17: p6, dec4, p3, (T4B, T4F) twice, p3, dec4, p6, 36 sts.

Row 18: k10, p2, k4, p4, k4, p2, k10.

Row 19: p9, T3B, p4, C4B, p4, T3F, p9.

Row 20: k9, p2, k5, p4, k5, p2, k9.

Row 21: p8, T3B, p3 T4B, T4F, p3, T3F, p8.

Row 22: k8, p2, (k4, p2) 3 times, k8.

Row 23: p8, (k2, p4) 3 times, k2, p8.

Row 24: rep row 22.

Row 25: rep row 23.

Row 26: rep row 22.

Row 27: p8, T4F, p2, T4F, T4B, p2, T4B, p8.

Row 28: rep row 18.

Rep rows 1–28 for patt.

BACK

Using 4 mm needles and M/C, cast on 80 (92-100-108-112) sts. Work 2 rows in seed st. Then place cable panel as follows:

RS row: k22 (28-32-36-38), work RS set-up row of chart, k22 (28-32-36-38).

WS row: p22 (28-32-36-38), work WS set-up row of chart, p22 (28-32-36-38).

Next RS row: k22 (28-32-36-38), work row 1 of chart, k22 (28-32-36-38).

Next WS row: p22 (28-32-36-38), work row 2 of chart, p22 (28-32-36-38).

Cont working chart rows in sequence with panel as now set, until back measures 14 (14-14.5-15-15.5) in [35.5 (35.5-37-38-39.5) cm] from beg, end RS row facing for next row.

shape sides as follows:

RS row: k1, inc in next st, patt to last 2 sts, inc in next st, k1.

WS row: p1, inc in next st, patt to last 2 sts, inc in next st, p1.

Rep these 2 rows 7 (7-8-9-10) more times, take all inc sts in St St, 112 (124-136-148-156) sts.

shape raglans as follows:

Note: when checking st count during raglan shaping, cable panel reads as 36 sts, therefore disregard the inc sts within panel for overall st count.

Cont in patt dec 1 st at each end of every following RS row 32 (26-24-20-20) times, 48 (72-88-108-116) sts rem.

WS row: work even in patt. Then dec 1 st at each end of every row 6 (18-26-36-40) times, 36 sts rem.

work hood extension as follows:

Cont working cable panel as set on rem 36 sts until hood extension measures 18 in [46 cm]. BO all sts.

RH FRONT

Using 4 mm needles and M/C, cast on 40 (46-50-54-56) sts and work 2 rows in seed st. Then place cable panel as follows:

RS row: k2 (5-7-9-10), work RS set-up row of chart, k2 (5-7-9-10).

WS row: p2 (5-7-9-10), work WS set-up row of chart, p2 (5-7-9-10).

Next RS row: k2 (5-7-9-10), work row 1 of chart, k2 (5-7-9-10).

Next WS row: p2 (5-7-9-10), work row 2 of chart, p2 (5-7-9-10).

Cont working chart rows in sequence with panel as now set, until front measures 14 (14-14.5-15-15.5) in [35.5 (35.5-37-38-39.5) cm] from beg, end RS row facing for next row. ***

shape side as follows:

RS row: patt to last 2 sts, inc in next st, k1.

WS row: p1, inc in next st, work in patt to end.

Rep these 2 rows 7 (7-8-9-10) more times, take all inc sts in St St, 56 (62-68-74-78) sts.

shape raglan and front neck as follows:
Cont in patt throughout

RS row: work to last 3 sts, k2tog, k1 (this is raglan edge).

WS row: work even in patt.

Rep these last 2 rows 24 (24-23-19-19) more times.

Then dec 1 st at raglan edge every row 0 (0-2-12-10) times, 31 (37-42-42-48) sts rem.

All sizes RS row: BO 5 (4-4-4-5) sts, work in patt to last 3 sts, k2tog, k1.

S and M sizes, WS row: work even in patt.

L, XL, and 2X sizes, WS row: p1, p2tog, work in patt to end.

All sizes, RS row: BO 5 (4-4-4-5) sts at beg of next row, work in patt to last 3 sts, k2tog, k1. Rep last WS row as given for size above.

S size only: dec 1 st at both raglan and neck edges on next 6 RS rows, 7 sts rem.

M, L, XL, and 2X sizes only: dec 1 st at both raglan edge and neck edge on following 8 (8-8-6) rows, 11 (14-14-22) sts rem.

All sizes: cont, dec 1 st at raglan edge every row, keeping neck edge even, until 3 sts rem. K3tog, break off yarn and draw through loop.

LH FRONT

Work as given for RH front until beg of side shaping, marked ***, end with RS row facing for next row.

shape side as follows:

RS row: k1, inc in next st, work in patt to end.

WS row: patt to last 2 sts, inc in next st, p1.

Rep the 2 rows 7 (7-8-9-10) more times, take all inc sts in St St, 56 (62-68-74-78) sts.

shape raglan and front neck as follows:
Cont in patt throughout,

RS row: (this is raglan edge) k1, k2togb, patt to end.

WS row: work even in patt.

Rep these last 2 rows 24 (24-23-19-19) more times.

Then dec 1 st at raglan edge every row 0 (0-2-12-10) times, 31 (37-42-42-48) sts rem.

Next row (RS): k1, k2togb, patt to end.

All sizes WS row: BO 5 (4-4-4-5) sts, work in patt to last 3 sts, p2togb, p1.

S and M sizes: work RS row even.

L, XL, and 2X sizes RS row: k1, k2togb, work in patt to end.

All sizes: WS row: BO 5 (4-4-4-5) sts at beg of next row, work in patt to last 3 sts, p2togb, p1. Rep last RS row as given for size above.

S size only: dec 1 st at both raglan edge and neck edges on next 6 RS rows, 7 sts rem.

M, L, XL, and 2X sizes only: dec 1 st at both raglan and neck edge on following 8 (8-8-6) rows, 11 (14-14-14-22) sts rem.

All sizes: cont dec 1 st at raglan edge every row, keeping neck edge even until 3 sts rem. P3tog, break off yarn and draw through loop.

SIDE PANELS (MAKE 2 ALIKE)

Using 4 mm needles and Color A, cast on 36 (36-42-48-54) sts, work 2 rows in seed st. Then beg with a knit row, work in St St until piece measures 14 (14-14.5-15-15.5) in [35.5 (35.5-37-38-39.5) cm] from beg, end RS row facing for next row.

shape sides as follows:
cont working in St St, dec 1 st at each end of next 12 (12-14-17-19) rows, 12 (12-14-14-16) sts rem.

Next row: (RS) k2togb, k2, BO next 4 (4-6-6-8) sts, k2, k2tog.

WS row: p2tog, p1, turn, k2tog, break off yarn and draw through loop. Rejoin yarn to rem 3 sts,

WS row: p1, p2tog, turn, k2tog, break off yarn and draw through loop.

SLEEVE (MAKE 2 ALIKE)

Using 4 mm needles and Color A, cast on 62 sts, work 2 rows in seed st.

place cable panel as follows:
RS row: k13, work RS set up row of chart, k13.

WS row: p13, work WS set up row of chart, p13.

Next RS row: k13, work row 1 of chart, k13.

Next WS row: p13, work row 2 of chart, p13.

Cont working chart rows in sequence with panel as now set, *at the same time* inc 1 st at each end of row 5 (5-3-3-3) and every following 6th (6-6-4-4) row 15 (14-23-2-11) times, 94 (92-110-

68-86) sts. Work all incs sts in St St throughout. Then cont in patt inc 1 st at each end of every following 8th (8-0-6-6) row 5 (6-0-22-16) times, 104 (104-110-112-118) sts. Work even until sleeve measures 18 (18.5-18.5-19-19) in [46 (47-47-48-48) cm] from beg.

shape raglans as follows:
Note: when checking st count during raglan shaping, cable panel reads as 36 sts. Therefore, disregard the inc sts within panel for overall st count.

Cont in patt BO 6 sts at beg of next 2 rows. Then dec 1 st at each end of every RS row 35 (35-37-38-40) times. Leave rem 22 (22-24-24-26) sts on a st holder.

FINISHING AND HOOD

Weave in ends. Block all pieces to given dimensions.

Sew zipper to CFs as follows: working on a flat surface (not your knee) lay the zipper behind the CF opening with zipper teeth along edges. Pin in place, then using a contrasting sewing thread and taking great care not to stretch or pucker the fabric, baste the zipper in place using a running stitch. Remove pins. Now, using matching sewing thread, whipstitch the zipper tape to the WS of each front. Then working on RS approx 1 st away from edge, stitch zipper in place using matching sewing thread and backstitch. Remove basting.

Sew side panels to fronts and backs, matching lower edges and side shapings. Sew all 4 raglan seams, matching bound off sts at beg of sleeve raglan shapings to top of side panels. Sew sleeve seams.

LHS hood:
Using 4 mm needles and M/C, with RS facing and beg at back of LHS sleeve, knit 22 (22-24-24-26) sts from sleeve st holder, then pick up and knit 28 (28-28-30-32) sts down LHS front neck, 50 (50-52-54-58) sts total.

WS: k5, purl to end.

RS: knit all sts.

Rep these 2 rows until piece measures 10.5 in [26.5 cm], end RS row facing for next row.

shape top as follows:
Dec 1 st at beg of next row. Dec 1 st at end of following row. BO 2 sts at beg of next row. Work WS row even. BO 4 (4-4-4-6) sts at beg of next row. Work WS row even. BO 6 (6-8-10-12) sts at beg of next row. Work WS row even. BO 12 sts at beg of next row. Rep the last 2 rows once more. Work WS row even. BO rem 12 sts.

RHS hood:
Using 4 mm needles and M/C, with RS facing and beg at CF, pick up and knit 28 (28-28-30-32) sts up RHS front neck, then knit 22 (22-24-24-26) sts from RH sleeve st holder, 50 (50-52-54-58) sts total.

WS: purl to last 5 sts, k5.

RS: knit all sts.

Rep these 2 rows until piece measures 10.5 in [26.5 cm], end WS row facing for next row.

shape top as follows:

Dec I st at beg of next row. Dec I st at end of following row. BO 2 sts at beg of next row. Work RS row even. BO 4 (4-4-4-6) sts at beg of next row. Work RS row even. BO 6 (6-8-10-12) sts at beg of next row. Work RS row even. BO 12 sts at beg of next row. Rep the last 2 rows once more. Work RS row even. BO 7 sts. Cont working on rem 5 sts in garter st (knit every row), until extension measures 4.5 in [11.5 cm]. BO. Sew sides of hood to each side of cable panel extension of back. Stitch garter extension (RHS hood) to BO edge of cable panel to neaten front edge of hood. Press lightly, following the instructions on the yarn label.

mindfulness pointer: row by row

This is not a difficult cable, but it is not easily memorized, so it will require concentration. Therefore, you need to be disciplined in working it. Take pleasure in the commitment it requires, as the monks must have done in their work. It breaks down into small units, so you will find that it is not too demanding to work a set number of repeats each time you sit down to knit. Then, little by little, its beauty will come to fruition. This is not necessarily an instant gratification project—it's not supposed to be. I hope that you will find that the joy of making it is in its gradual materialization.

peek-a-boo

In our culture, we are bombarded with messages telling us to take time to relax and unwind. I find it strange that we need to be reminded to do this.

We usually don't need to be reminded not to put ourselves in danger, so why do we need to be reminded to take care of ourselves? Besides, taking time for ourselves is something pleasurable rather than a chore, so it should be an easy sell. After all, no one has to spend much time encouraging me to eat chocolate or to knit. We have become conditioned to feel guilty if we are not always achieving something.

Is knitting so popular because it is both relaxing and productive? In days gone by, knitting was only ever seen as work. Today, we understand both its meditative aspect and its ability to induce relaxation.

I designed this sweater with the long, lazy days of summer in mind, when you sit under a tree and kick back. It is designed for both making and wearing on such days. With this in mind, the cable is simple to learn and will transport you easily into a relaxed state. The pattern contains two variations of the same cable, one filled, one empty, reminding us to follow our breath as we work; breathe in, breathe out. Finally, to add a sense of fun, the cables have peek-a-boo holes at the neckline and cuffs.

SIZES / FINISHED CHEST MEASUREMENTS

Small 36 in [91.5 cm]
Medium 39 in [99 cm]
Large 42 in [106.5 cm]
XL 46 in [117 cm]
2X 50 in [127 cm]

Instructions are given for smallest size. If changes are necessary for larger sizes, the instructions are given in ( ). Where there is only one set of figures, this applies to all sizes.

MATERIALS

Svale by Dale of Norway shade 0010, 13 (14-15-16-18) 50 g balls, (50% cotton–10% silk–40% viscose).

Pair of 4 mm needles, 24 in [61 cm]-long circular 3.5 mm needle used for neckband, 3.25 mm needle (used for neckband bind off), 1 stitch holder, CN.

Yarn amounts given are based on average requirements and are approximate.

TENSION / GAUGE

28 sts and 32 rows = 4 in [10 cm] over cable pattern with 4 mm needles.

25 sts and 32 rows = 4 in [10 cm] over rev St St with 4 mm needles.

Take the time to check your gauge; change needle sizes if necessary to obtain correct gauge and garment size.

REFER TO GLOSSARY ON PAGE 13 FOR: SEED STITCH.

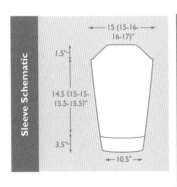

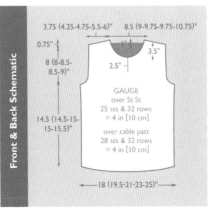

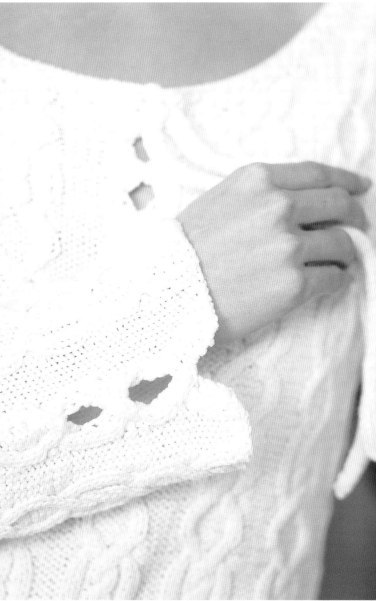

- [⊡] p on RS; k on WS
- [□] k on RS; p on WS

C4B

C4F

T4B

T4F

Chart reads R to L RS rows and L to R WS rows

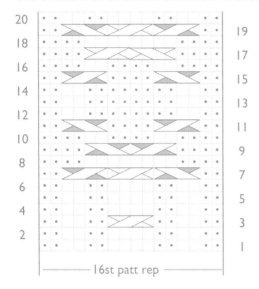

|— 16st patt rep —|

Please see note on placing markers in
Things You Need to Know Before You Begin (p.8)

CABLE PATTERN

Row 1: (RS) p2, k2, p2, k4, p2, k2, p2.

Row 2: k2, p2, k2, p4, k2, p2, k2.

Row 3: p2, k2, p2, C4B, p2, k2, p2.

Rows 4–6: rep row 2, then rows 1 and 2 once more.

Row 7: p2, T4F, C4B, T4B, p2.

Row 8: k4, p8, k4.

Row 9: p4, T4B, T4F, p4.

Row 10: (k4, p2) twice, k4.

Row 11: p2, T4B, p4, T4F, p2.

Row 12: k2, p2, k8, p2, k2.

Row 13: p2, k2, p8, k2, p2.

Row 14: rep row 12.

Row 15: p2, T4F, p4, T4B, p2.

Row 16: rep row 10.

Row 17: p4, C4F, C4B, p4.

Row 18: rep row 8.

Row 19: p2, T4B, C4B, T4F, p2.

Row 20: rep row 2.

Rep rows 1–20 for patt.

BACK

With 4 mm needles, cast on 126 (136-148-160-174) sts, work 2 (2-6-6-10) rows in seed st. Then place pattern as follows:

(RS) p7 (12-18-8-15), work row 1 of chart 7 (7-7-9-9) times, p7 (12-18- 8-15).

(WS) k7 (12-18-8-15), work row 2 of chart 7 (7-7-9-9) times, k7 (12-18-8-15).

Cont working chart rows in sequence as set until piece measures approx 14.5 (14.5-15-15-15.5) in [37 (37-38-38-39) cm] from beg, end with row 7 of patt facing for next row.

shape armhole as follows:

Cont in patt, BO 4 sts at beg of next 2 rows. Then BO 3 sts at beg of following 2 rows, 112 (122-134-146-160) sts rem. Work even in patt until armhole measures 8 (8-8.5-8.5-9) in [20 (20-21.5-21.5-23) cm] from beg of shaping. Make a note of this row so that you can match shoulder shaping on front.

shape shoulders and back neck as follows:

BO 9 (10-11-13-14) sts at beg of next row, patt across until there are 21 (23-25-29-31) sts on RH needle (inc st on needle after BO), turn, leave rem 82 (89-98-104-115) sts on a spare needle.

Working only on the 21 (23-25-29-31) sts, BO 2 sts at beg of next row, work in patt to end.

Next row (RS): BO 9 (10-11-13-14) sts at beg of row, work to end.

WS row: BO 1 st at beg of row, work to end.

RS: BO rem 9 (10-11-13-14) sts.

Return to sts on spare needle, slip center 52 (56-62-62-70) sts onto a stitch holder. Rejoin yarn and work to end, 30 (33-36-42-45) sts.

Next row (WS): BO 9 (10-11-13-14) sts at beg of row, work in patt to end.

RS row: BO 2 sts at beg of row, work to end. Next row: BO 9 (10-11-13-14) sts, work to end.

RS row: BO 1 st at beg of row, work to end. BO rem 9 (10-11-13-14) sts.

FRONT

Work as given for back until completion of armhole shaping. Work 8 rows even in patt, end having worked row 18 of chart.

work peek-a-boo opening as follows:
Note: work with 2 balls of yarn but do not twist them around each other, you are forming an opening in the center of the cable.

******RS row:** p0 (5-11-1-8), work as given row 19 of chart 3 (3-3-4-4) times, place marker, p2, T4B, work C4B knitting first 2 sts with ball #1 and joining ball #2 for the last 2 sts, T4F, p2, place second marker, work as given row 19 of chart 3 (3-3-4-4) times, p0 (5-11-1-8).

Cont in patt over cable panels at each side, *at the same time* working CF cable panel, between markers, as follows:

WS row: k2, p3, p3togb. Using ball #1, p3tog, p3, k2, 4 sts dec at CF.

Row 1: p2, k2, k2tog. Using ball #2, k2togb, k2, p2, further 2 sts dec at CF.

Row 2: k2, p3. Using ball #1, p3, k2.

Row 3: p2, k3. Using ball #2, k3, p2.

Row 4: k2, p2, purl into front and back of next st. Using ball #1, purl into front and back of next st, p2, k2, 2 sts inc at CF.

Row 5: p2, k2, p1, knit into front and back of next st. Using ball #2, knit into front and back of next st, p1, k2, p2, further 2 sts inc at CF.

Row 6: k2, p2, k2, knit into front and back of next st. Using ball #1, knit into front and back of next st, k2, p2, k2, further 2 sts inc at CF.

Row 7: p2, T4F, then using ball #2, work C4B with last 2 sts from 1st side and first 2 sts from 2nd side, twist yarns around one another to prevent hole, then working across rem sts from 2nd side T4B, p2.

Row 8: work as given row 8 of chart twisting yarns around each other at center point. ***

Row 9: p4, C4B. Using ball #2, C4F, p4.

Note: now work each side separately without twisting yarns around each other.

Row 10: k4, p2, p2togb. Using ball #1, p2tog, p2, k4, 2 sts dec at CF.

Row 11: p2, C4B, k1. Using ball #2, k1, C4F, p2.

Row 12: k2, p2, p3togb. Using ball #1, p3tog, p2, k2, further 4 sts dec at CF.

Row 13: p2, k3. Using ball #2, k3, p2.

Row 14: k2, p2, purl into front and back of next st. Using ball #1, purl into front and back of next st, p2, k2, 2 sts inc at CF.

Row 15: p2, slip next 2 sts onto CN and hold at front of work, p into front and back of next st from LH needle, k2 from CN, knit into front and back of next st. Using ball #2, knit into front and back of 1st st, slip next st onto CN and hold at back of work, k2 from LH needle, p into front and back of st on CN, p2, further 4 sts inc at CF.

Row 16: work as given row 16 of chart, twisting yarns around each other at center point.

Rows 17 and 18: Using ball #1, work across all sts in patt. Break off ball #2.

shape LHS front neck as follows:
Cont in patt as set (next row will be row 19 of chart), work across 46 (51-57-63-70) sts, turn, (this is neck edge) leave rem 66 (71-77-83-90) sts on a spare needle.

Next row: (WS) BO 6 sts at beg of row, patt to end. Work RS row even.

WS: BO 4 sts at beg of row, patt to end.

Rep the last 2 rows 1 (1-2-2-3) more times, 32 (37-39-45-48) sts rem. Work RS row even.

Next row (WS): BO 2 sts at beg of row, patt to end. Work RS row even.

Rep the last 2 rows 1 (2-2-2-2) more times. Then dec 1 (1-0-0-0) st at neck edge on following row, 27 (30-33-39-42) sts rem.

Work even until you reach the same row as back before shoulder shaping, end RS row facing for next row.

BO 9 (10-11-13-14) sts at beg of next row. Work WS row even.

Rep the last 2 rows once more. BO rem 9 (10-11-13-14) sts.

Return to sts on spare needle. Rejoin yarn, BO center 20 sts.

shape RHS front neck as follows:
Work across rem 46 (51-57-63-70) sts in patt (row 19 of chart) as set.

Next row (WS): work to end in patt.

RS row: BO 6 sts at beg of row, patt to end. Work WS row even.

RS row: BO 4 sts at beg of row, patt to end.

Rep the last 2 rows 1 (1-2-2-3) more times, 32 (37-39-45-48) sts rem. Work WS row even.

Next row (RS): BO 2 sts at beg of row, patt to end. Work WS row even.

Rep the last 2 rows 1 (2-2-2-2) more times. Then dec 1 (1-0-0-0) st at neck edge on following

row, 27 (30-33-39-42) sts rem.

Work even until you reach the same row as back before shoulder shaping, end WS row facing for next row.

BO 9 (10-11-13-14) sts at beg of next row. Work RS row even.

Rep the last 2 rows once more. BO rem 9 (10-11-13-14) sts.

SLEEVE (MAKE 2 ALIKE)

Work 1st side of cuff as follows:

With 4 mm needles, cast on 35 sts, work 2 rows in seed st.

RS row: p13, work row 1 of chart, p2, k4.

WS row: k2, p2, k2, work row 2 of chart, k13.

Cont in patt as set, working edges as above and cable patt rows in sequence until row 5 of chart has been worked.

Row 6: k into front and back of both first 2 sts, p2, k2, work row 6 of chart, k13.

Leave these 37 sts on a spare needle. Leave yarn attached.

Using ball #2, work 2nd side of cuff as follows:

With 4 mm needles, cast on 35 sts, work 2 rows in seed st.

RS row: k4, p2, work row 1 of chart, p13.

WS row: k13, work row 2 of chart, k2, p2, k2.

Cont in patt as set work edges as

above and cable patt rows in sequence until row 5 of chart has been worked.

Row 6: k13, work row 6 of chart, k2, p2, k into front and back of both last 2 sts, 37 sts.

Return to first side of cuff and work as follows:

RS: working sts from 1st side of cuff, p13, work as given row 7 of chart once, p2, T4F, then using ball #2, work C4B with last 2 sts from 1st side and first 2 sts from 2nd side, twist yarns around each other to prevent hole, then working across rem sts from 2nd side, T4B, p2, work as given row 7 of chart once, p13, 74 sts.

Row 8: k13, work row 8 of chart 3 times, k13.

Row 9: p13, work row 9 of chart once, p4, C4B. Using ball #2, C4F, p4, work row 9 of chart once, p13.

Note: work with 2 balls of yarn but do not twist them around one another; you are forming an opening in the center of the cable.

Row 10: k13, work row 10 of chart once, k4, p2, p2togb. Using ball #1, p2tog, p2, k4, work row 10 of chart once, k13, 72 sts.

Row 11: p13, work row 11 of chart once, p2, C4B, k1. Using ball #2, k1, C4F, p2, work row 11 of chart once, p13.

Row 12: k13, work row 12 of chart once, k2, p2, p3togb. Using ball

#1, p3tog, p2, k2, work row 12 of chart once, k13, 68 sts.

Row 13: p13, work row 13 of chart once, p2, k3. Using ball #2, k3, p2, work row 13 of chart once, p13.

Row 14: k13, work row 14 of chart once, k2, p2, knit into front and back of next st. Using ball #1, knit into front and back of next st, p2, k2, work row 14 of chart once, k13, 70 sts.

Row 15: p13, work row 15 of chart once, p2, slip next 2 sts onto CN and hold at front of work, p into front and back of next st from LH needle, k2 from CN, knit into front and back of next st. Using ball #2, knit into front and back of 1st st, slip next st onto CN and hold at back of work, k2 from LH needle, p into front and back of st on CN, p2, work row 15 of chart once, p13, 74 sts.

Row 16: k13, work row 16 of chart 3 times, twisting yarns around each other at center point, k13.

Rows 17 and 18: work across all sts in patt as set.

Cont in patt over cable panels on each side, *at the same time* working 2nd peek-a-boo hole opening in center cable panel. Work this panel as given from *** to *** on front. Break off ball #2.

Now working across all sts throughout, beg working from row 9 of chart for all cable panels. Cont working in patt, *at the same time* inc 1 st at each end of row 11 and every following 6th (8-6-6-4) row 2 (13-13-14-7) times, 80 (102-102-104-90) sts, work all inc sts in rev St St throughout. Then inc 1 st at each end of every following 8th (0-8-8-6) row 11 (0-3-3-13) times, 102 (102-108-110-116) sts. Work even in patt until piece measures 18 (18.5-18.5-19-19) in [46 (47-47-48-48) cm], from beg, end RS row facing for next row.

shape cap as follows:

Cont in patt as set, BO 4 sts at beg of next 2 rows and 3 sts at beg of following 2 rows. Then dec 1 st at each end of next 8 rows. BO rem 72 (72-78-80-86) sts.

FINISHING AND NECKBAND

Weave in ends. Block all pieces to given dimensions. Join both shoulder seams.

With RS facing, using circular 3.5 mm needle, cast on 65 sts. K65, then beg at CF, pick up and knit 50 sts up RHS front neck, then pick up and knit 8 sts down RHS back neck, knit across 52 (56-62-62-70) sts from back neck stitch holder dec 10 sts evenly across these sts, pick up and knit 8 sts up LHS back neck, then pick up and knit 50 sts down LHS front neck, 158 (162-168-168-176) sts around neck +65 sts for tie.

Working back and forth, cast on 65 sts at beg of next row (WS), p65, work in seed st to last 65 sts, p65. RS row: k65, work in seed st to last 65 sts, k65. WS row: p65, work in seed st to last 65 sts, p65. Rep last 2 rows once more. Using 3.25 mm needle, BO all sts.

Set in sleeves to armholes. Join side seams. Cross ties over each other at CF and stitch in place. Press lightly, following the instructions on the yarn label.

mindfulness pointer: marking time

If you are like most knitters, you probably prefer to put your knitting down once you reach a particular point in the pattern, like reading to the end of a novel's chapter. But with knitting there are more options for stopping—it could be the end of a row or a pattern repeat. Try experimenting, stop at the same point in a pattern every time when working on one piece, then stop at a different point each time on another piece. Does one way feel easier? Which way adds to the relaxation and enjoyment your knitting brings you?

index of projects and yarns

change

nature

energy

 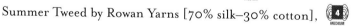
time

yarn suppliers

ALAFOSS LETT-LOPI

available from JCA Inc.

CASCADE YARNS

www.cascadeyarns.com
1-800-548-1048
1224 Andover Park East
Tukwila, WA 98188

CLASSIC ELITE YARNS

www.classiceliteyarns.com
1-800-343-0308
122 Western Ave.
Lowell, MA 01851

DALE OF NORWAY

www.dale.no
1-800-441-3253
N16 W23390 Stoneridge Dr.
Ste A
Waukesha, WI 53188
in Canada available from Estelle
Designs

DIAMOND YARNS

www.diamondyarn.com
1-800-268-1896
9697 St. Lauren, Ste 101
Montreal, QC H3L 2N1 Canada
or
115 Martin Ross, Unit #3
Toronto ON M3J 2L9 Canada

ECO KNIT

available from Infiknit

ESTELLE DESIGNS

www.estelledesigns.ca
1-800-387-5167
Units 65/67 2220 Midland Ave.
Scarborough ON M1P 3E6
Canada

HEMP YARN

available from Infiknit

INFIKNIT

www.infiknit.com
1-800-408-1522
542 Mt Pleasant Rd., unit 104
Toronto ON M4S 2M7 Canada

JCA INC

1-800-225-6340
35 Scales Ln.
Townsend, MA 01469

KING COLE YARNS

available from Cascade Yarns
in Canada available from Estelle
Designs

MISSION FALLS

www.missionfalls.com
1-800-209-0597
PO Box 224
Consecon ON K0K 1T0 Canada
in USA available from Unique
Kolours Ltd

NEEDFUL YARNS

www.needfulyarnsinc.com
1-866-800-4700
4476 Chestwood Dr., Unit 10-11
Toronto ON M3J 2B9 Canada

NATURALLY YARNS

available from S.R. Kertzer

ROWAN YARNS

www.rowanyarns.co.uk
available from Westminster Fibers
in Canada available from Diamond Yarns

SHELRIDGE FARMS

www.shelridge.com
1-866-291-1566
RR #2 Ariss,
ON N0B 1B0 Canada

S.R. KERTZER

www.kertzer.com
1-800-263-2354
50 Trowers Rd.
Woodbridge, ON
L4L 7K6 Canada

SWEATERKITS

www.sweaterkits.com
1-877-232-9415
PO Box 397
Sharon ON L0G 1V0 Canada

UNIQUE KOLOURS LTD

www.uniquekolours.com
1-800-252-3934
28 N. Bacton Hill Rd.
Malvern, PA 19355

WESTMINSTER FIBERS

www.knitrowan.com
1-800-445-9276
4 Townsend West, Unit 8
Nashua, NH 03063

acknowledgments

Although writing a book is a highly personal experience, it is far from being a solitary one. Several people have given a great deal in terms of many hours of work and of themselves by way of their own personal expertise. Without their input, this book would have been an impossible task. I owe them the huge debt of gratitude. I hope that they already know how much I value not only their contributions but also the emotional support they extended to me.

Many thanks to the yarn companies and distributors who generously provided yarn. Special thanks to Caroline, Susan, Chris, Mags, Kathy, Josie, Elizabeth, Carol, Ted, and Buffy, who aided in selecting the best product for each project. Test knitters: Joan Kass, Carole Herbert, Sandra Whittaker, Susan Preston, Wannietta Prescod, Sandi Proser for their skill and tireless effort. Joan thanks for your continuous support. Technical editor, Gayle Bunn, for her eagle eyes. Graphic designer, Rebecca Cober, for her patience and enthusiasm. Photographer Lindsey Maier for her creativity and talent. My agent Linda Roghaar, my editor Rosy Ngo, and the team at Potter Craft for believing in me. I reserve my final and most special thanks for the man who is always standing right behind me urging me on in everything I do, but who was even more spectacular than I could have ever dreamed a husband to be while I worked on this book: Rob, I love you!

My heartfelt thanks to all of you!

index